150 Boise Icons

150 Boise Icons

TO CELEBRATE THE CITY'S SESQUICENTENNIAL

BY ANNA WEBB

AN IDAHO STATESMAN PUBLICATION

The icons in this book are divided into four chapters by geographic region. The book includes a chronological table of contents as well as alphabetical and categorical indexes. Each icon is numbered, includes an address and is color-coded to its corresponding map.

FROM THE COLLECTION OF MARK BALTES

Main Street near 9th, circa 1910.

Pioneer Tent & Awning Building

The Pioneer Tent & Awning Co. operated for 70 years in Downtown Boise. Its sign, a white horse, still prances over 6th and Main.

Fourth-generation Boisean John Davidson nominated the building as a Boise icon. The company was still in business when he was a child.

"It was a magical place for a teenage boy. I'd go there simply to touch the smells. The aroma of leather and canvas greeted me at the door. They stocked tents and saddles, awnings, all kinds of camp gear. Tack for spirited steeds and trail-toughened mules were staples carried in bulk," wrote Davidson.

PHOTO BY DARIN OSWALD

DID YOU KNOW? *Pioneer Tent & Awning's white horse sign, an icon in its own right, dates to at least 1918. The city nearly lost it. After Pioneer Tent went out of business, the owners sold the horse at auction. It ended up at a local antique store. Longtime Boise store owner Hugh Angleton tracked it down. Angleton had it refurbished and returned to its proper place, where it remains today.*

76 THE BOISE ICONS

Thanks to our partners — the Boise City Department of Arts and History, Preservation Idaho and Icon Credit Union — for helping the Idaho Statesman publish this book.

Foreword

By Anna Webb

PHOTO BY DARIN OSWALD

Anna Webb's favorite icon is the Old Ada County Courthouse. Her father, Jay Webb, argued his first cases there as a public defender in the 1960s.

The year 1863 was a big one for Boise. President Abraham Lincoln made Idaho a territory. The U.S. Army founded Fort Boise. A group of pioneers met at a cabin not far from where the Grove Plaza is today and platted the city's original 10 blocks.

The Idaho Statesman published its first paper from a dirt-floor cabin on Main Street a year later.

The paper, with its deep roots in the city, wanted to mark Boise's 150th anniversary in a fitting way. We decided to run a series of short stories about 150 places and things that make Boise the city it is.

We asked readers to submit their ideas to fill out a list of local "icons." They answered the call with everything from the profound (the Idaho State Capitol), to the quirky (the Vista Washer Woman), to the environmental (the Foothills), to the comedic (finger steaks, invented in Boise, some say).

Historians at Preservation Idaho helped round out the list with sites that played a part in Boise's evolution from 10 blocks sketched out by hand to the metropolis it became by 2013.

Our icon series, a mix of the new, the old and the offbeat, focused on public places that people can visit, on things they can see or experience — even eat in a few cases.

The series ran for 150 consecutive days beginning in February. It ended with the city's birthday celebration on July 7 in Julia Davis Park.

My icon research proved to be more interesting and elicited more hometown pride than I'd expected. Buildings I've driven past a hundred times revealed fascinating pasts. The understated Reclamation Building on Broadway was the nerve center for massive dam projects. The O'Farrell Cabin, the city's oldest residence, has its original fireplace and its cottonwood walls. The Assay Office on Main Street hasn't changed much since the days when Idaho was still a territory.

The series stirred readers' passions and opinions. In many cases, readers wrote to share their connections to places such as C.W. Moore Park and the Pioneer Building. Some of those anecdotes are included in this book.

The piece on vintage drive-in restaurants brought in more emails than any other icon. Readers wanted to weigh in about beloved lost eateries such as Murray's, the Frostop, the Howdy Pardner. Who knew fast food held such a spot in Boiseans' hearts?

Other icons hit a nerve. The piece about finger steaks inspired an anonymous caller to tell me in no uncertain terms that icons are historic statues and buildings, certainly not finger steaks. The piece about the Marian Pritchett School led one reader to send me a picture of a Byzantine Madonna. The latter, not

NO. 49. JULIA DAVIS PARK DRIVE ENTRANCE, BOISE, IDAHO

the former, is an icon, said the reader.

What was heartening, even if readers disagreed about the definition of icon, was that this city and all its stories matter deeply to the people who live here.

Historian Judy Austin, a valued adviser to me on many occasions, pointed out her favorite definition of icon from the Oxford English Dictionary: "A person or thing regarded as a representative symbol of a culture, movement, etc."

This book is a compilation of the symbols of our local culture, as it stands in our sesquicentennial year.

RAIN MAKER'S

RUSSELL FOTO
252.

CARNIVAL, BOISE
IDA.

SCHOOL CHILDREN IN PARADE

Letter from Mayor David Bieter

Everyone who loves Boise has a Boise icon that's near and dear.

Some are skyline-defining landmarks: the Idaho State Capitol, the Boise Depot. Some harken from our city's earliest days as a pioneer community: Fort Boise, the O'Farrell Cabin. From the natural geological wonder of Table Rock to the whimsical local kitsch of the Vista Washer Woman, our city is adorned with monuments and curiosities of every kind — relics from the past, talismans of the present and signposts to the future.

As Boise celebrates its sesquicentennial as a city in 2013, Idaho Statesman writer Anna Webb has met the challenge of cataloging 150 of the icons that help to define this remarkable place — and to define us as well. I've lived in this city virtually my whole life, and almost every one of Anna's stories revealed something I didn't know.

If our BOISE 150 commemoration has taught us anything, it's that history is a continuous process; we are destined to keep on inventing it. So consider this book not just a tribute but a challenge: to create more Boise icons that will spark the imaginations and warm the hearts of generations to come.

Gora Boise!

David H. Bieter
Mayor

Schoolchildren march on Main Street near 10th in a parade for the City of Boise's 50th anniversary in 1913.

FROM THE COLLECTION OF MARK BALTES

Letter from John Bertram, Preservation Idaho

This publication illustrates the wealth of Boise's historic resources and offers a glimpse into what the city is all about. The icons enumerated here tell us about ourselves and possess a charm and quality that cannot be easily duplicated.

Founded in 1972, Preservation Idaho's advocacy efforts have helped to save numerous sites from the wrecker's ball. We have rallied support to protect and preserve icons such as the historic Old Ada County Courthouse, The Cabin, Bar Gernika on the Basque Block, the Empire Building and the Bown House, which serves as a history center for Boise's fourth-graders. With a mission of preserving Idaho's historic places through collaboration, education and advocacy, our efforts to protect Boise's icons continue. Such work often finds preservationists seeming to stand alone during challenging times, with few early supporters.

But once saved, the buildings become appreciated landmarks and unique symbols of our city; a source of pride and part of the economic engine that drives Boise's prosperity.

Preservation Idaho remains committed to safeguarding historic resources and recognizing the importance of the past. By bringing together enthusiastic and dedicated groups of citizen volunteers, we can ensure that Boise continues to reap the benefits of the preservation of a century and a half of history.

The 150 Boise Icons, along with all our historic buildings, are a manifestation of our conviction that historic preservation is integral to our economic development. They bring positive attention to our community, remind us of who we are and who we have been, and reinforce the promise of livability and cultural richness for all our citizens.

Thanks to reporter Anna Webb and the Idaho Statesman, the 150 Boise Icons series built a daily appreciation of Boise as we prepared to honor her July 7, 2013, sesquicentennial. We trust that they will be preserved and cherished for another 150 years. Enjoy the icons of Boise.

Sincerely,

John Bertram
Preservation Idaho President

IDAHO'S FAMOUS NATATORIUM,
BOISE, IDAHO

Icon Timeline

Bonneville Point
PAGE 191

Oregon Trail
PAGE 196

1830

1840

1850

Foote
Homesite
PAGE 192

Stone Steps and
Hitching Posts
PAGE 229

Warm Springs
Avenue
PAGE 224

YMCA
PAGE 20

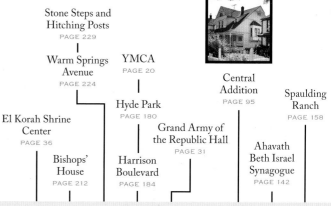

Central
Addition
PAGE 95

Spaulding
Ranch
PAGE 158

Hyde Park
PAGE 180

El Korah Shrine
Center
PAGE 36

Grand Army of
the Republic Hall
PAGE 31

Ahavath
Beth Israel
Synagogue
PAGE 142

Bown House
PAGE 202

Morris Hill Cemetery
PAGE 140

Bishops'
House
PAGE 212

Harrison
Boulevard
PAGE 184

1880

1890

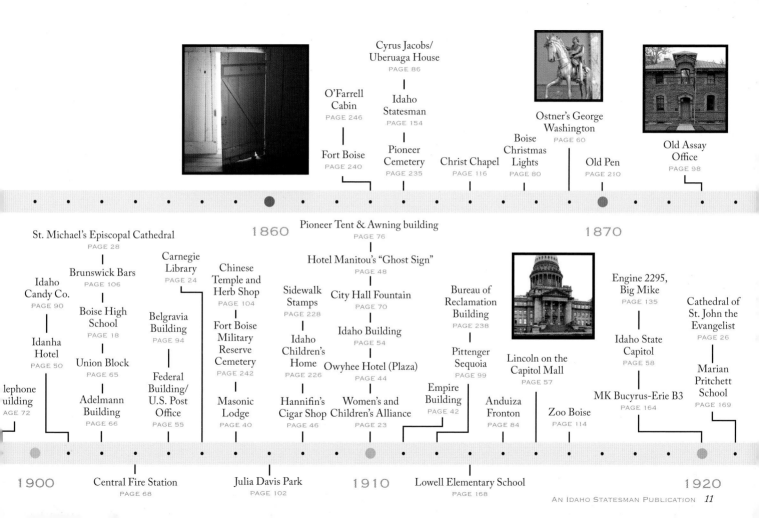

Cyrus Jacobs/
Uberuaga House
PAGE 86

O'Farrell
Cabin
PAGE 246

Idaho
Statesman
PAGE 154

Ostner's George
Washington
PAGE 60

Fort Boise
PAGE 240

Pioneer
Cemetery
PAGE 235

Christ Chapel
PAGE 116

Boise
Christmas
Lights
PAGE 80

Old Pen
PAGE 210

Old Assay
Office
PAGE 98

1860

1870

Pioneer Tent & Awning building
PAGE 76

St. Michael's Episcopal Cathedral
PAGE 28

Hotel Manitou's "Ghost Sign"
PAGE 48

Brunswick Bars
PAGE 106

Carnegie
Library
PAGE 24

Chinese
Temple and
Herb Shop
PAGE 104

Sidewalk
Stamps
PAGE 228

City Hall Fountain
PAGE 70

Bureau of
Reclamation
Building
PAGE 238

Engine 2295,
Big Mike
PAGE 135

Idaho
Candy Co.
PAGE 90

Boise High
School
PAGE 18

Belgravia
Building
PAGE 94

Fort Boise
Military
Reserve
Cemetery
PAGE 242

Idaho
Children's
Home
PAGE 226

Idaho Building
PAGE 54

Pittenger
Sequoia
PAGE 99

Cathedral of
St. John the
Evangelist
PAGE 26

Idaha
Hotel
PAGE 50

Union Block
PAGE 65

Owyhee Hotel (Plaza)
PAGE 44

Lincoln on the
Capitol Mall
PAGE 57

Idaho State
Capitol
PAGE 58

lephone
uilding
AGE 72

Federal
Building/
U.S. Post
Office
PAGE 55

Masonic
Lodge
PAGE 40

Hannifin's
Cigar Shop
PAGE 46

Women's and
Children's Alliance
PAGE 23

Empire
Building
PAGE 42

Anduiza
Fronton
PAGE 84

Zoo Boise
PAGE 114

MK Bucyrus-Erie B3
PAGE 164

Marian
Pritchett
School
PAGE 169

Adelmann
Building
PAGE 66

1900

Central Fire Station
PAGE 68

Julia Davis Park
PAGE 102

1910

Lowell Elementary School
PAGE 168

1920

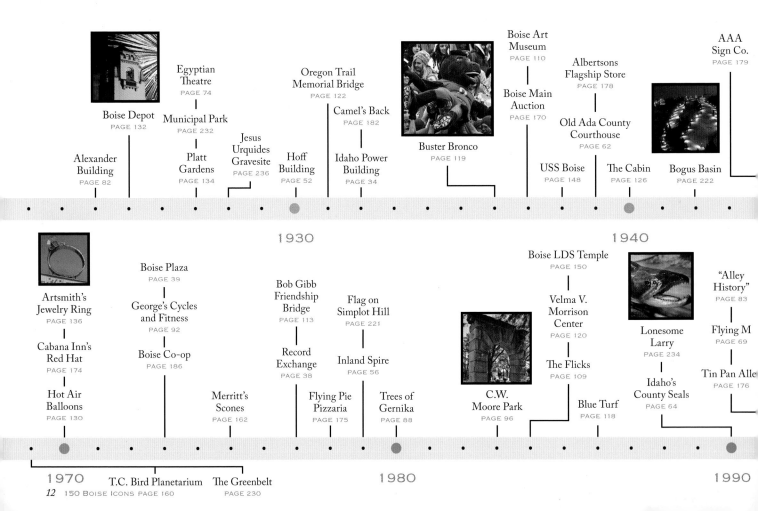

Boise Art
Museum
PAGE 110

AAA
Sign Co.
PAGE 179

Egyptian
Theatre
PAGE 74

Oregon Trail
Memorial Bridge
PAGE 122

Albertsons
Flagship Store
PAGE 178

Boise Main
Auction
PAGE 170

Boise Depot
PAGE 132

Municipal Park
PAGE 232

Camel's Back
PAGE 182

Old Ada County
Courthouse
PAGE 62

Alexander
Building
PAGE 82

Platt
Gardens
PAGE 134

Jesus
Urquides
Gravesite
PAGE 236

Hoff
Building
PAGE 52

Idaho Power
Building
PAGE 34

Buster Bronco
PAGE 119

USS Boise
PAGE 148

The Cabin
PAGE 126

Bogus Basin
PAGE 222

1930

1940

Boise LDS Temple
PAGE 150

Boise Plaza
PAGE 39

"Alley
History"
PAGE 83

Velma V.
Morrison
Center
PAGE 120

Artsmith's
Jewelry Ring
PAGE 136

George's Cycles
and Fitness
PAGE 92

Bob Gibb
Friendship
Bridge
PAGE 113

Flag on
Simplot Hill
PAGE 221

Lonesome
Larry
PAGE 234

Flying M
PAGE 69

Cabana Inn's
Red Hat
PAGE 174

Boise Co-op
PAGE 186

Record
Exchange
PAGE 38

Inland Spire
PAGE 56

The Flicks
PAGE 109

Tin Pan Alle
PAGE 176

Hot Air
Balloons
PAGE 130

Merritt's
Scones
PAGE 162

Flying Pie
Pizzaria
PAGE 175

Trees of
Gernika
PAGE 88

C.W.
Moore Park
PAGE 96

Blue Turf
PAGE 118

Idaho's
County Seals
PAGE 64

1970

T.C. Bird Planetarium

The Greenbelt

1980

1990

150 BOISE ICONS PAGE 160

PAGE 230

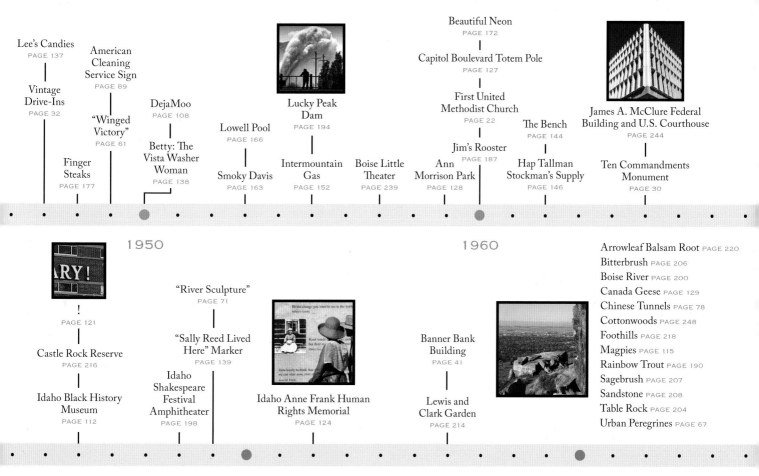

Lee's Candies
PAGE 137

Vintage
Drive-Ins
PAGE 32

Finger
Steaks
PAGE 177

American
Cleaning
Service Sign
PAGE 89

"Winged
Victory"
PAGE 61

DejaMoo
PAGE 108

Betty: The
Vista Washer
Woman
PAGE 138

Lowell Pool
PAGE 166

Smoky Davis
PAGE 163

Lucky Peak
Dam
PAGE 194

Intermountain
Gas
PAGE 152

Boise Little
Theater
PAGE 239

Beautiful Neon
PAGE 172

Capitol Boulevard Totem Pole
PAGE 127

First United
Methodist Church
PAGE 22

Jim's Rooster
PAGE 187

Ann
Morrison Park
PAGE 128

The Bench
PAGE 144

Hap Tallman
Stockman's Supply
PAGE 146

James A. McClure Federal
Building and U.S. Courthouse
PAGE 244

Ten Commandments
Monument
PAGE 30

1950

1960

RY!
!
PAGE 121

Castle Rock Reserve
PAGE 216

Idaho Black History
Museum
PAGE 112

"River Sculpture"
PAGE 71

"Sally Reed Lived
Here" Marker
PAGE 139

Idaho
Shakespeare
Festival
Amphitheater
PAGE 198

Idaho Anne Frank Human
Rights Memorial
PAGE 124

Banner Bank
Building
PAGE 41

Lewis and
Clark Garden
PAGE 214

2000

2010

Eighth Street looking north. Above: circa 1910. Below: circa 1955.

Main Street. Above: Looking west, circa 1910. Below: Looking east, circa 1957.

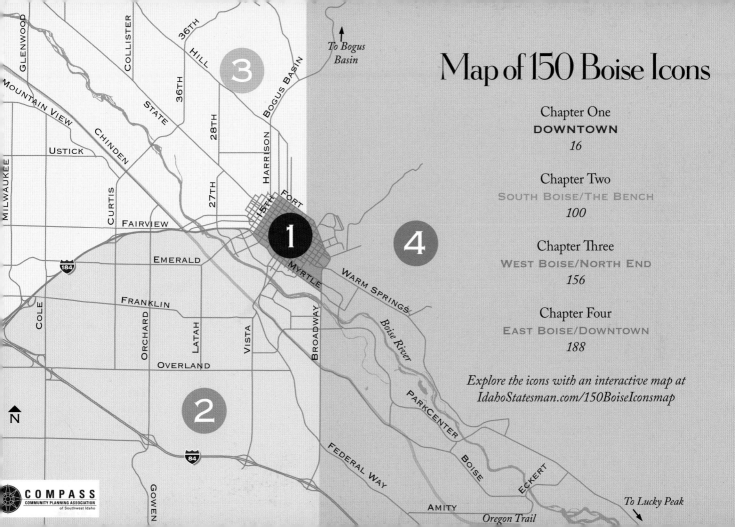

Map of 150 Boise Icons

Explore the icons with an interactive map at
IdahoStatesman.com/150BoiseIconsmap

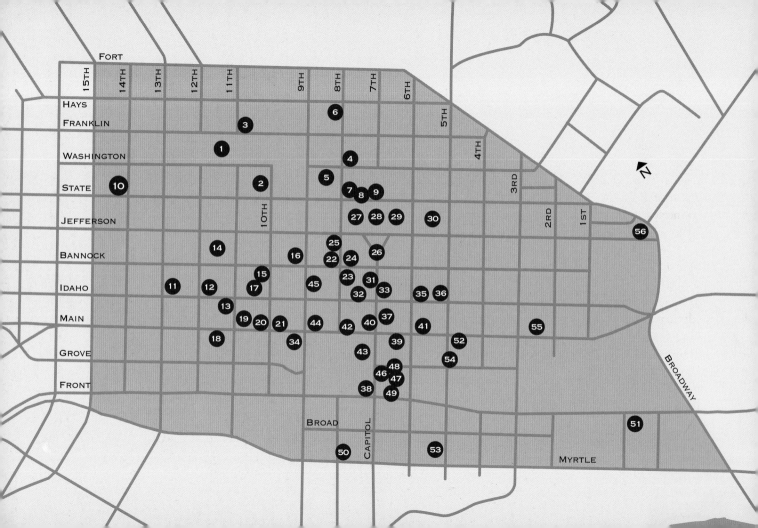

Chapter One DOWNTOWN

Boise High School

The School District built Boise High in 1902 on the site where the central portion of the school now stands. District leaders proclaimed that the red brick building was large enough to accommodate Boise students "for all time."

But in 1908, the district hired the architectural firm Tourtellotte and Hummel to add the first of many expansions, a white brick addition to the building's east side. In 1912, it added a white brick addition to the west side. The addition of a white stucco Industrial Arts building (on the site of the current library) came in 1919. In 1922, the district replaced the original red brick central building with the white three-story structure that anchors the school today.

PHOTO BY DARIN OSWALD

DID YOU KNOW? *Boise High's many architectural decorations include lion-headed rain spouts. And that's a bust of Plato gazing down from the school's pediment.*

The school got its Art Deco-style gym in 1936, a contemporary of the Hotel Boise a few blocks away. Like the Boise Art Museum and the Old Ada County Courthouse built in the same era, the gym was a New Deal project. According to one account, students saved their own money to contribute to the project.

Fans of Deco style should be sure to note the decorative sunburst panels near the gym's roofline. The school added a modern music building on the west side of the gym in 1957.

The school is now a kind of architectural tour through the ages. Upgrades in the late 1990s meant the loss of the Industrial Arts building (and its art studios, auto and print shops), but the school's Neoclassical main building is intact, Ionic columns and all.

The school has many claims to fame: Bing Crosby and Duke Ellington performed in its

Boise High School, Boise, Idaho

Boise High School's original building, 1902.

auditorium. Boise's first radio station transmitted its signal from the school roof in the 1920s. Like many historic Boise buildings, BHS is heated with geothermal water.

Construction of Boise's other traditional public high schools followed in the next decades: Borah in 1958 and Capital in 1964. Timberline opened in 1998.

YMCA

The YMCA might have buildings and programs across the Treasure Valley these days, but everything started in a considerably more modest way. Boisean Walter Bruce founded Boise's first Y in a single room in the Sonna Block on Main Street in 1891.

A small church note in the Statesman in 1893 includes a listing for the YMCA: "If sinners entice thee, consent thou not, but come to the Y."

Jim Everett, CEO of the Treasure Valley Family YMCA, said the organization first opened in England in 1844. It was a time when young men were leaving the countryside and moving to cities to look for work. Cities meant temptations such as bars and brothels. Early Y founders wanted to provide a Christian-based alternative.

The first American Y opened in

PHOTO PROVIDED BY TREASURE VALLEY YMCA

DID YOU KNOW? *The Y's second building (no longer standing) was at 11th and Idaho. Note the sign for the "Boise Servicemens Lounge." Returning troops frequently found lodging at Y's. The old building meant a lot to Bill Barrett. In 1951, he was a young soldier stationed at Gowen Field. A fellow soldier talked him into going to a USO dance at the Y. He walked in, heard "Stardust" playing in the ballroom upstairs, and saw a girl in a polka-dot blouse walking down the stairs. "It was love at first sight," said Barrett. He and his wife, Lorraine, that girl in polka dots, have been together more than 60 years. When the Y tore the building down, Barrett salvaged a brick.*

Boston in 1851. Western migration carried the Y across the country.

The Y at 10th and State is the organization's third building in Downtown Boise (not counting that room on Main Street).

Leaders laid the cornerstone of the first building on the northeast corner of 10th and Grove streets in the summer of 1901 (about the same time the Idanha Hotel opened for business). The Y organized baseball and basketball teams and even offered a tennis court on Main Street between 12th and 13th streets.

The organization continued to grow. It opened camps for boys on Payette Lake. It moved into its second building in the summer of 1920 on the northwest corner of 11th and Idaho streets.

Boise's early Y's included residences for men. A lot of military personnel returning from service stayed at Y's while they transitioned back into civilian life, said Everett.

FUNDSY, the local philanthropic group that celebrated its 45th anniversary in 2012, came together in 1967 to support capital improvements at the Y.

The Y dedicated its current building at 10th and State in 1968.

"Some of our members have been with us for so long they still call this 'the new Y,'" said Everett.

The organization struggled financially during the 1960s, he said. It sold its Payette Lake camp to help pay for the new building. A capital campaign in 1983 raised the money to pay off the 1968 project as well as other expansions and renovations.

The Y's evolutions have included changing sensibilities. For many decades, the men's locker room was considerably larger than the women's. Programs for women were limited.

"Now we like to say we're the most inclusive place in the Valley,"

PHOTO BY DARIN OSWALD

said Everett.

It's not uncommon to see a bank president and a young woman from Interfaith Sanctuary using treadmills next to one another.

The Y broke ground for its Camp at Horsethief Reservoir in 2007, replacing the camp it had to sell in the 1960s. The Y celebrated the completion of its main lodge at Horsethief, the final building project at the camp, in the city's sesquicentennial year.

First United Methodist Church

This church was built between 1958 and 1960. Boiseans may know it by its other name, Cathedral of the Rockies.

In the city's sesquicentennial year, the church welcomed a new addition — a set of "herald trumpets" for its existing pipe organ. The trumpets, long pipes that extend horizontally from the wall, increase the size of the organ, which is already the largest of its kind in the state. They also increase its volume. No other church in the state has similar trumpets.

Congregation member Lavaughn Wells gave the trumpets in memory of her late husband, David Wells, founder of the Blue Thunder Marching Band at Boise State University.

The church's publicity team came up with the term "herald trumpets" to help people visualize the rows of long, flared horns used to mark the arrival of royalty, said congregation member Sue Myers.

The church, though new in historic terms, is home to a far older congregation: It began meeting in 1872, less than a decade after the city's founding.

The building is "cruciform," or cross-shaped. As the Banner Bank building is a modern interpretation of Art Deco style, First United Methodist is a modern take on Gothic style.

When the church underwent renovation some years ago, the local quarry that provided the original sandstone reopened so the additions would match.

The church's stained-glass windows include notable figures such as George Washington, Confederate Gen. Robert E. Lee and others

IDAHO STATESMAN FILE

DID YOU KNOW? *The church's carillon bells that peal out on crisp mornings, lending a collegiate feel to the North End, are not actually bells. They're digital and operate on a timer.*

not usually associated with religious imagery. Each had a tie to the Methodist denomination.

Women's and Children's Alliance

At the turn of the 20th century, Boise boasted lively streets. Tall buildings, including the Idanha Hotel and the new State Capitol, were springing up. Growth and job prospects lured people to the city from rural areas. The rush created a housing shortage and potentially dangerous situations — especially for young women of modest means.

According to "Women Helping Women," a book by Sarah Nash celebrating the Women's and Children's Alliance's centennial in 2011, a group of young, forward-thinking women came together to improve their living conditions. By 1911, they had formed the Young Women's Christian Association of Boise.

After visiting the city, Francis Gage, general secretary of the national YWCA for the Northwest, said, "Boise has already done an unusual thing, in that the call for this organization has come from the girls themselves and not from the prominent women of the city."

Some of those well-heeled women soon joined the cause. The group became affiliated with the national organization. It opened a boarding house and cafeteria in the McCarty Building at 9th and Idaho.

The organization settled into its current home in 1940. It became many things for many people — residence, cafeteria, crisis center, classroom, gym, thrift store. It housed the city's first homeless day shelter. During World War II, more than 40 community groups used the building as a meeting place.

Today, its mission is providing safety, healing, and freedom from

PHOTO BY ANNA WEBB

DID YOU KNOW? *The organization's name changed from YWCA to WCA in 1996, after a decision to allow men on the board forced a break with the national organization.*

domestic abuse and sexual assault, remaining true to those women who hoped for good lives a century ago.

Carnegie Library Building

Like more than 2,500 other cities, Boise got its first dedicated library building thanks to steel magnate Andrew Carnegie. The Carnegie name is still visible on the Classical Revival building's facade.

But the women of the Columbian Club, one of Boise's oldest — and still active — service clubs, had a lot to do with it. Libraries were clearly dear to the women's hearts. In 1895, they established Boise's first library and reading room in City Hall.

When the philanthropic Carnegie program began, it required cities to guarantee matching funds to maintain libraries after they were built. Columbian Club members lobbied city leaders to get that guarantee.

The Carnegie Library opened in

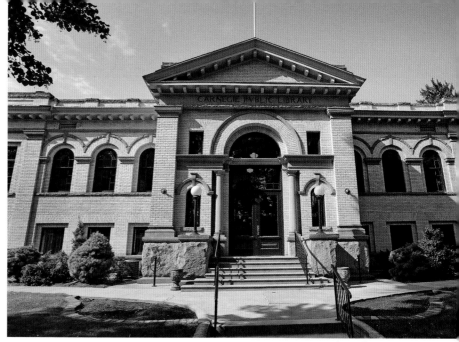

IDAHO STATESMAN FILE

DID YOU KNOW? *In addition to money from Andrew Carnegie, local contributions and a land donation from the Boise School District made the library possible.*

the summer of 1905. Hundreds of Boiseans turned out to celebrate and hear speeches by dignitaries at the Columbia Theater.

The Idaho Statesman wrote, "It is

perhaps not generally understood by the public that when this library is opened the circulating department as well as the reading room will be absolutely free to the citizens of Boise."

Two hundred and fifty residents signed up for library cards immediately. Borrowers were allowed two books at a time — one fiction, one nonfiction.

The public library remained in the Carnegie building for seven decades.

In 1973, the library moved to today's location, the former Salt Lake Hardware building on Capitol Boulevard. City leaders decided that buying and renovating the hardware building was more cost-effective than tearing down the old library and rebuilding on Washington Street.

Today St. Michael's owns the Carnegie Library building. A law firm and several organizations keep offices there.

The library's fireplace, complete with frieze of horses and riders, is still intact, along with the original circulation desk. The dumbwaiter that once lifted books from the basement is gone.

PHOTO BY JOE JASZEWSKI

DID YOU KNOW? *Dreamy, color-saturated murals painted by Olaf Moller in the 1930s remain in the basement, the former children's book area. A mural of a prince with a page boy haircut approaching a reclining woman on a beach hangs in the ladies room. A painting of Neptune in his underwater kingdom hangs in the office of the Idaho Academic Decathlon.*

Cathedral of St. John the Evangelist

By 1893, just three years after President Benjamin Harrison signed Idaho into statehood, the state's Catholic community had grown to approximately 7,000 parishioners.

Around that time, The Most Reverend Alphonse Glorieux, bishop of the newly established Diocese of Boise, recognized the need for a cathedral in the capital city.

The diocese bought the 8th Street block where St. John's sits today. It hired Boise architects Tourtellotte and Hummel to design the cathedral in 1904. Builders laid the cornerstone in 1906.

According to "Shaping Boise: A Selection of Boise's Landmark Buildings," published by the city's planning department, the diocese built the cathedral in sections as money became available.

Architect Charles Hummel I (grandfather of architect Charles Hummel, who still lives in Boise) was a member of Boise's Catholic community. He intended the church's imposing square towers to be gothic-style steeples.

Lack of funding cut that plan — and the towers — short. It also meant the church remained a solidly Romanesque structure with rounded arches, thick massive walls and a sense of solidity.

Builders finished the cathedral's roof and walls in 1912. They sometimes borrowed equipment from the Capitol building construction project going on nearby. Church services took place in the cathedral's basement.

Church leaders dedicated the cathedral on Easter 1921.

Luke McIntosh, 11, a fifth-grader

at St. Joseph's Catholic School, nominated St. John's as an icon.

"The stained glass windows are very detailed and cool. I go to church there every Tuesday with my school where I learn about Catholicism thanks to the awesome priests Father Henry and Father Brian," Luke wrote.

His favorite window? That featuring St. Alphonsus. It's bright and colorful, Luke said.

Builders installed the cathedral's windows in 1920, with the exception of the modern Holy Spirit window directly above the high altar. Builders installed it during a 1979 renovation.

An example of history coming full circle: Charles Hummel oversaw the renovation of the church his grandfather designed, continuing the family's deep ties to the building.

27

St. Michael's Episcopal Cathedral

The cathedral marked its first century in 2002. The Gothic Revival building is made of local sandstone and opened its doors in 1902 to an overflow crowd of 500.

That congregation had long outgrown its original home, the small white church now known as Christ Chapel, that has sat beside Bronco Stadium since the 1960s.

The history of St. Michael's is interwoven with the history of the city and Boise State.

The Episcopal Church founded St. Margaret's Hall, a school for girls, in Boise in 1892. St. Michael's Bishop Middleton Barnwell converted the school into Boise Junior College — forerunner of Boise State University — in the 1930s. Not only did Barnwell write the curriculum, but he also built the benches for the school's science lab.

Just months after the dedication of the cathedral in 1902, St. Michael's Bishop James Funsten opened St. Luke's Hospital with six beds.

The St. Michael's Women's Auxiliary supported the hospital by making bandages and dressings for surgery, furnishing patient rooms, sewing layettes for the nursery and buying lab equipment, according to a church history written by Eve Chandler.

On the lighter side, St. Michael's is also responsible for the city's Music Week tradition. The cathedral's organist, Eugene Farner, began the annual program in 1919.

DID YOU KNOW? *St. Michael's owns two of the most significant historical sites in Downtown Boise: the old Carnegie Library and the G.A.R. Hall just east of the cathedral.*

PHOTO BY JOE JASZEWSKI

When you visit, note the baptismal font hewn from local sandstone with the inscription "Suffer little children to come unto Me." Children in the church raised money to buy the font in 1869. Other special features include a stone in the church's east transept from the National Cathedral and a nativity stained-glass window, also in the east transept, signed by Louis Tiffany around 1918.

Ten Commandments Monument

This monument's presence in a Boise park prompted questions about the separation of church and state and the proper role of city government.

The Fraternal Order of Eagles donated the monument to the city in 1965. City leaders installed it in Julia Davis Park between the band shell and the Boise River.

Long before the controversy, the monument had quite a story. A Minnesota Fraternal Order of Eagles official started a campaign in the 1950s to print and disseminate the Ten Commandments throughout Minnesota.

At that time, Cecil B. DeMille was working on his "Ten Commandments" Hollywood epic. He contacted the Eagles and suggested expanding their Commandments program to coincide with the film. DeMille

advocated for more permanent Ten Commandments markers.

The Eagles agreed, and sponsored 167 monuments — including Boise's — across the country.

Boise's monument stood for nearly four decades, overlooked for the most part, in its shady corner of the park. But in 2003, some began to question whether the religious monument belonged on city land.

This attracted the attention of an out-of-state religious group that wanted to put up its own themed memorial in Boise next to the monument. Boise Mayor David Bieter and the City Council hoped to circumvent the controversy. The council voted to remove the Ten Commandments from the park and return it to the Fraternal Order of Eagles.

The vote inspired protests, vigils

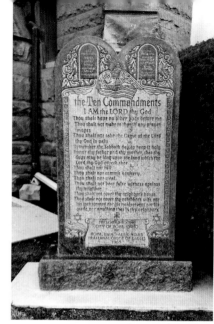

PHOTO BY ANNA WEBB

DID YOU KNOW? *Boiseans approved moving the monument to St. Michael's in a 2006 ballot initiative.*

and talks of recalling the mayor and council members. St. Michael's Episcopal Church offered a solution: moving the monument to its front lawn. It stands there today.

Grand Army of the Republic Hall

After the Civil War, thousands of veterans from both sides moved west, according to the Idaho State Historical Society. About 1,000 settled in Idaho. Boise has its own remnants of the conflict. One of the most notable: the G.A.R. Hall north of the Idaho State Capitol.

Members of the Grand Army of the Republic, a fraternal organization for veterans of the Union Army, U.S. Navy, Marines and Revenue Cutter Service, built the hall in 1892.

They named it for Union Gen. Philip Sheridan. Sheridan is known for defeating Confederate forces in the Shenandoah Valley through the use of scorched-earth tactics.

The University of Idaho now has offices in the hall, but the G.A.R. insignia remains on the facade.

While you're in the neighborhood, walk across the street to the lawn of the state Capitol. You'll find another G.A.R. monument "lovingly erected and dedicated by the ladies of the Grand Army of the Republic."

They dedicated the monument in 1935, 70 years after the war ended — the same span of time that now separates us from World War II.

Statesman reader Linda Channel said that her father, Charles M. Wilson, engraved the words on the stone. Wilson worked for the Jellison Monuments company.

"He only had one eye and attended school only to the fourth grade. The wording on the monument is very long and he must have done the engraving very carefully to spell everything correctly," said Channel.

Idaho's last living Civil War veteran, Israel Broadsword, died in 1952.

PHOTO BY ANNA WEBB

DID YOU KNOW? *Memorial Park at Fort and 6th streets is dedicated to the Grand Army of the Republic. A plaque on a large stone not far from the federal courthouse reads, "Erected by Idaho Society in 1926. This park is dedicated to the G.A.R., which preserved the Union 1861-1865."*

Vintage Drive-Ins

Boise, never a city to shy away from fun, especially fun related to both eating and cars, still has its share of independent drive-ins.

It seems important, though, to take a minute to note the drive-ins we've lost. Everyone had a favorite. And passions run deep.

In the mid-1970s, Chow Now on Broadway Avenue sold ice cream sandwiches as thick as old-school leather wallets, with both chocolate and vanilla ice cream inside. It took your whole walk home from school to eat one.

The College In-N-Out on University Drive was the place to go for a Bronco Burger or cherry dipper bar, a cool vanilla medallion encased in vermillion shellac. The Historical Society has the drive-in's big wooden menu in storage.

There are other lost greats, including the Frostop on Fairview. It got so busy on weekends in the 1960s that its owners hired off-duty police officers to direct traffic. The Smoke Inn out on State Street was famous for its turkey nuggets. Murray's, which sat in what's BoDo today, had its loyal fans. The Howdy Pardner had dancing ladies on its roof. Kids liked to drive back and forth between the latter two until late in the night.

Happily, many of Boise's vintage purveyors of fries, tots and finger steaks remain. Like neon signs, they represent an aspect of the city's popular, commercial culture that distinguishes it from anywhere else.

Speaking of neon, Fanci Freez's neon ice cream cone glows on State Street. A classic Boise sight worth seeking out if you never have: the neon cone with a full moon looming in the sky behind it.

Fanci Freez opened in 1947. Its most famous offering may be the Boston Shake, a combination shake and sundae. Its sister restaurant, Big Bun on Overland Road, opened in 1961.

Hawkins Pac-Out opened on Bogus Basin Road in 1954. Its signature menu item is the Herby Burger. That's Herby himself, the burger with the biceps, on the drive-in's sign. Hawkins employee Dan McAuliffe, pointed out Herby's sidekicks, a milkshake and a packet of fries. Both wear red lipstick.

"They've been around forever," he said.

The Westside Drive-In on State Street started out as a grocery store in the 1930s. It converted to a drive-in

in 1957, said its owner Chef Lou Aaron. The Westside, which has a second location on ParkCenter Boulevard, is known for finger steaks. But Chef Lou has the trademark on another treat: the Ice Cream Potato. The chef at the now-closed Gamekeeper Restaurant made the first ice cream potatoes — balls of ice cream dusted with cocoa and covered in whipped cream — in the 1940s, said Aaron. He made his first in 1978.

The Viking Drive-In opened in the early 1960s on State Street. The Moore family has owned it since 1974. House specialty? "The Henderson." It's on the menu now, but it used to be an item you had to know to ask for. The burger was named for a customer who still patronizes The Viking, said Julie Moore.

"It has double everything — meat, cheese, ham and six pieces of bacon," said Moore.

Viking philosophy from Moore: "We do everything as old school as possible."

Idaho Power Building

The architectural firm Wayland & Fennell designed Idaho Power Co.'s headquarters in 1932. The Art Deco style it exemplifies swept the U.S. at the height of the Machine Age between the World Wars. America embraced speed and industrialization on a grand style. The Idaho Power building's vertical lines and geometrical, angular ornamentation reflect all of this.

"What better way to show that you are a modern enterprise than to promote and incorporate modern architecture into your headquarters?" said Dan Everhart of Preservation Idaho. "The building is representative of its time and the value that Idaho Power executives placed on being perceived as modern and bold."

Idaho Power added a 50-foot extension to the building's east side in 1960. This expansion has raised questions in the preservation community because it's seamless. It's impossible to tell where the old building ends and the new building begins — to some preservationists, that's a misrepresentation.

But there's no controversy about the company's more recent, painstaking restoration of the building's exterior paint, said Everhart. Rather than using abrasives that could harm the decorative surface, restorers applied a kind of chemical peel, then repainted. The distinctive Art Deco chevrons — that may or may not be an homage to Reddy Kilowatt and his electric bolt limbs — appear as crisp as they must have in the '30s.

Idaho Power was created in 1916 when five companies across southern Idaho and Oregon combined assets,

PHOTO BY ANNA WEBB

DID YOU KNOW? *One of the best features of the exterior, looking a bit like a set design from a gangster movie or the grill of a Gatsby roadster, is the company's gleaming name plate. Aluminum is commonplace now, but in the 1920s and 30s, it was the hot new architectural metal, a glamorous harbinger of the future.*

including water rights and hydroelectric facilities on the Snake River. The company built the majority of its hydroelectric facilities in the years after the Idaho Street headquarters

Idaho Power's Idaho Street headquarters in the 1970s.

was built, leading up to the completion of the three-dam Hells Canyon Complex in 1968.

Idaho Power constructed its new headquarters on the block south of the original building in 1990. The company uses the 1932 building for office space. An underground tunnel connects the two.

El Korah Shrine Center

Boise's El Korah Shriners got their charter in 1898 — making them as much of a city icon as their temple.

The Shriners are a national charitable fraternal organization that began in 1870, born out of a group of Masons who met regularly for cocktails in New York City.

They decided the Masons were too focused on ritual, so they created their own group devoted to fun and fraternity. The 13 founding Shriners adopted the fezzes and Near Eastern theme "on a lark," said Potentate Ron Lester of the Boise Shrine Center.

All Shriners are Masons, but not all Masons are Shriners.

By 1920, the national Shriners organization adopted the welfare

PHOTO BY JOE JASZEWSKI

DID YOU KNOW? *Historic as it is, the El Korah Shrine Center is no static time capsule. It was one of the venues for the Treefort Music Fest in 2013.*

of children as its charitable cause. The group opened its first Shriners hospital, which is still operating, in Shreveport, La.

Today, members raise money for

the 22 Shriners hospitals across the U.S. No child needing medical care is turned away for lack of funds, said Lester.

The local organization's building

on Idaho and 12th streets dates to the late 1800s.

Its first use was as a city livery stable. A fire in 1913 gutted the building; 55 horses perished. The Shriners, who had been holding their meetings and ceremonies at the Natatorium, at a 10th Street skating rink and the First National Bank building, rebuilt the damaged stable in 1914. They built an addition in 1928.

There's a lot more than meets the eye at the Shrine Center. The Shriners' band room still has its 1920s light fixtures. The Oasis bar and restaurant in the basement serves lunch five days a week. Technically, guests are supposed to be accompanied by a member, but no one's likely to be turned away, said Lester.

An expansive ladies room at the temple earned a nod from Boise Weekly in 2009 as one of the finest bathrooms in the city (think plush pink carpet and a profusion of silk

EL KORAH TEMPLE   THE MOSQUE, BOISE, IDAHO   A. A. O. N. M. S.

FROM THE COLLECTION OF MARK BALTES

floral arrangements).

Another special feature: 11 murals with a desert theme painted by Boise sign-maker, muralist and Shriner J.H. Hopffgarten in 1921. The organization plans to restore them to their Jazz Age glory.

Next time you're in the neighborhood, stop by and ask a Shriner to show you Hopffgarten's framed case of jewels and ribbons from his time as potentate of the organization.

Record Exchange

To give you a sense of how long this Boise cultural icon has been around, when owner Michael Bunnell opened the store in 1977, Rod Stewart's "Tonight's the Night," Andy Gibb's "I Just Want to be Your Everything" and the Emotions' "Best of my Love" were among the most popular songs in America.

The Record Exchange did a brief stint in a small shopping mall on Orchard, then moved Downtown to the 100-year-old Hitchcock Building at the corner of 11th and Idaho, where it's been ever since. The sinister birds on the building's exterior are an homage to Alfred Hitchcock's 1963 film "The Birds."

All through Boise's revitalization in the 1970s and '80s — when

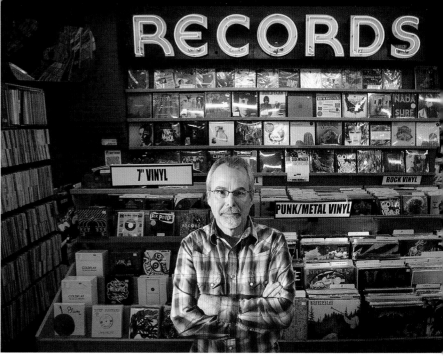

PHOTO BY KATHERINE JONES

DID YOU KNOW? *Record Exchange owner Michael Bunnell, executive director of the Coalition of Independent Record Stores, was one of the founders of National Record Store Day.*

the city's core was so desolate some likened it to a "free fire zone" — the Record Exchange provided a haven of music, life and color, "doing our thing somewhat doggedly," said longtime manager John O'Neil.

Boise Plaza

The building, home to Boise Cascade for more than 40 years, has another claim to fame. It was designed by the San Francisco office of the celebrated firm Skidmore, Owings and Merrill. That's the firm responsible for the Sears Tower (1973), which stood as the tallest building in the world for more than 20 years.

Skidmore, Owings and Merrill is notable for its early adoption of the sleek International Style (sometimes called the "glass box" style) that took off in the U.S. in the 1950s.

Think of the Lever House on Park Avenue in New York City, one of the first buildings to begin transforming the look of the avenue from heavy masonry to clean-line skyscrapers.

Those same clean lines are visible at Boise Plaza, built in 1971 to serve as Boise Cascade headquarters.

PHOTO PROVIDED BY RAFANELLI AND NAHAS

DID YOU KNOW? *The large lobby extends the full height of the building, with suspended walkways radiating from central elevator shafts to office space around the exterior of the building.*

Rafanelli and Nahas bought Boise Plaza in 2006. Boise Cascade and Boise Inc. still lease more than 60 percent of its space.

A few years ago, Rafanelli and Nahas led a nationwide search to find an artist to make a piece for the building. It chose Philadelphia artist Ray King. He installed "AquA" in 2010.

Consisting of more than 2,000 glass cubes that change color as the light shifts, the piece is the largest privately funded public art in the city.

Masonic Lodge

Nine Masonic organizations meet regularly at the historic 10th Street lodge in Downtown Boise.

Local Masons built it in 1906, making it a contemporary of St. John's Cathedral and the Turnverein Building, at 6th and Main. The fraternal organization expanded the building in 1920.

The building's numerous charms include a 1913 swamp cooler from New York City known affectionately as "Bertha." Bertha still works, thanks to regular oiling. A vault holds the sepia-toned photographs of lodge leaders from the turn of the last century.

The lodge once had a live-in custodian. His tiny apartment remains, uninhabited, on the top story. During World War I, the basement held an armory.

The community has used the lodge for various purposes over the past 90 years: funerals, fundraisers, polling during elections, and once, a bazaar featuring a palm reader named Queen Grizzella.

City historic preservation officials say the lodge is significant because of its constant use by one owner for nearly a century. Many of Boise's founding pioneers were Masons.

The 10th Street lodge is the Masons' fourth meeting place in Boise. The original temple was an adobe building at the corner of 7th and Idaho.

According to the Grand Lodge of Idaho website, there are about 4,000 Masons in the state today. Some historians say Freemasonry is the world's oldest fraternal organization, dating back to the late 14th century.

PHOTO BY JOE JASZEWSKI

DID YOU KNOW? *The Boise City Council voted to add the Masonic Lodge in Downtown Boise to its list of local historic landmarks in 2012. Becoming a landmark means the lodge joins iconic buildings such as the Old Ada County Courthouse and the Boise Depot. Lodge members petitioned for the honor, which comes with a brass plaque for the outside of the building.*

Banner Bank Building

Banner Bank, built in 2006, represents a modern take on Art Deco style. Geometric 1920s-style sheaves of wheat decorate its entrance. Despite that stylistic nod to an earlier era (echoed by its historic neighbor, the Hoff Building down the block), the Banner Bank is purely modern.

The bank is the first LEED platinum building in Idaho, the highest certification from the U.S. Green Building Council.

What does that mean in practical terms? The building uses 50 percent less energy than a traditional building. It's made from more than 40 percent recycled materials. Builders recycled more than 90 percent of the construction debris. Construction costs were on par with similar buildings using more standard building practices.

One cool touch: The building's exterior is made with as few parts as possible. The precast concrete panels essentially "snap" together. If anyone ever decides to use the Banner Bank's site for another purpose, they'll be able to unsnap the panels and use them again somewhere else.

Natural geothermal heat warms the building. Banner Bank is set up to harvest rainwater from the streets, sidewalks and surrounding parking lots. Graywater — wastewater from sinks and other washing facilities — flushes the toilets and urinals.

The building has motion sensors throughout that activate lights when people are around. Lighting also adjusts to the change of seasons. In the summer, when days are longer and brighter, interior lights dim accordingly.

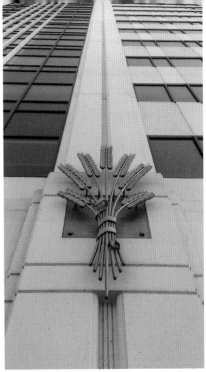

PHOTO BY ANNA WEBB

DID YOU KNOW? *When former Vice President Al Gore came to Boise in 2007 to give the keynote on global warming for the Frank Church Conference, the reception took place, appropriately, at the LEED-certified Banner Bank Building.*

Empire Building

The Kerr Hardware and Implement Co. built the Empire Building at 10th and Idaho streets between 1909 and 1911. Upon its completion, the Statesman reported that students of architecture considered the Empire the "handsomest building in the entire Northwest."

With its six stories, it was one of the tallest structures in Idaho until the 1930s, when buildings such as Hotel Boise surpassed it. Historians have noted its resemblance to the Wainwright Building in St. Louis (1891), considered one of the first skyscrapers in the world.

The firm Nisbet & Paradice designed Boise's Empire Building. The building has cousins — other designs by the same firm — including Sterry Hall at the College of Idaho, the original school for the blind in Gooding and a number of private residences.

The Empire features one of the most beautiful cornices (the top edge of the building) in town. Besides that cornice, echoed by the newer 9th and Idaho Center a block away, the most striking feature may be the entryway on the 10th Street side. Braced by Ionic columns, it reaches two full stories.

Grand as it was, the Empire hit a snag in 1919 when its owners had trouble finding tenants to occupy it. The Idaho Building on 8th Street attracted more renters, according to Preservation Idaho. The Empire's owners filed for bankruptcy. The First National Bank of Idaho bought the building at public auction. First National Bank grew. In 1927 it hired Tourtellotte and Hummel to build the Empire's smaller, white Neo-classical companion that still stands today on its west side.

The Empire faced a new threat in 1995. Then-owner West One Bancorp announced plans to tear it down and replace it with a public plaza. Preservation advocates and groups, including the National Trust for Historic Preservation, rallied to save it. A new owner, Tomlinson & Associates, renovated the building in 1999, earning an Orchid Award from Preservation Idaho. The renovation included reinforcing the building's posts and beams with a steel frame.

The foyer, its grandeur intact, still allows for a little time travel when you step inside. It might make you feel like getting your shoes shined and donning a fedora. Look up at the painted ceiling and take a sip from the old-style drinking fountain.

DID YOU KNOW? *The Empire Building is one of a trio of key Downtown buildings built around the same time. The Empire, along with the Idaho (1910) and Elks (1913) buildings, represent the beginnings of Boise's "skyscraper age," made possible by the advent of elevators a couple of decades earlier.*

Owyhee Hotel (Plaza)

The Owyhee, the city's second grand hotel, opened in Downtown Boise in 1910 — a decade after the Idanha's construction just up the street. The buildings remain two of Main Street's most notable historic structures.

Local businessmen Leo J. Falk and E.W. Schubert hired the Tourtellotte firm to design the Owyhee Hotel. Tourtellotte consulted with a Chicago design expert who urged him to increase the hotel's floors from four to six.

The opening of the hotel was a big event. Owners presented then-Gov. James Brady with a key. An ad in the Idaho Statesman claimed the Owyhee was the "most modern and complete commercial and tourist hotel between Chicago and San Francisco."

The original Owyhee had 125 guest rooms with mahogany furniture and what were then upscale amenities, including electric lights and connections to light switches so guests could plug in their curling irons. Guests could enjoy water from the hotel's artesian well.

Barbara Perry Bauer, a board member at Preservation Idaho, shared more details about the hotel's intriguing offerings:

"The Orange Room," decorated in shades of orange as its name suggests, had its own custom china and silver patterns.

Ladies sipped tea in "The Rose Grill," separate from the men who patronized the "beefsteak dungeon" downstairs. Candles lit this basement space. It featured a cell with a padlock for "obstreperous members."

The hotel also had a rooftop garden and dining area. Old postcard images show something reminiscent of the Hanging Gardens of Babylon — but with lanterns. The rooftop offered guests dramatic views of the Boise Foothills.

Idaho enacted statewide prohibition in 1916, but the Owyhee roof garden remained popular, wrote historian Arthur Hart. One could still enjoy "dancing, refreshments and music." And people still had to make reservations at what some billed as "The One Cool Spot in Boise" — cocktails or no.

The hotel continued to figure prominently in the life of the city. The Arid Club set up clubrooms there in 1934 during the Great Depression. The hotel added a new wing on its west side in the 1960s.

Major remodels in the late 1970s

ON THE OLD OREGON TRAIL.

425. OWYHEE HOTEL, BOISE, IDAHO.

DID YOU KNOW?

The Owyhee Hotel was a grand place, both with its imposing exterior and elegant interior. The gold stained-glass dome, removed from the lobby during the hotel's 1977 renovation, is now installed at the Idaho State Historical Museum.

FROM THE COLLECTION OF MARK BALTES

drastically altered the hotel's interior. The lobby lost its stained-glass dome and its mezzanine level with iron railing.

In the city's sesquicentennial year, the hotel was in the midst of another renovation, this time to convert it to apartments and office spaces and to reopen its rooftop garden.

Hannifin's Cigar Shop

A French pioneer named Edmund Salmon opened a tobacco business on 8th Street in the late 1800s. John B. Hannifin started working there in 1907 when he was just 11 years old. Salmon moved his store to its current location at Main and 11th in 1908. Hannifin bought the operation in 1919. He became what his granddaughter Jonni O'Neal called a "true tobacconist."

In its heyday, Hannifin's carried 125 brands of cigars.

John Hannifin later partnered with his brother Lawrence to run the shop. Lawrence Hannifin eventually became its sole owner.

Statesman columnist Tim Woodward interviewed a 96-year-old Boisean, George Emerson, in 1999.

DID YOU KNOW? *Hannifin's took a hit in the 1960s when the Cuban revolution curtailed the supply of Cuban cigars. For a time, Jerry Hannifin, John's son and a Time magazine correspondent, could source the cigars under the radar through his Latin American contacts. Pictured here: John Hannifin behind the counter.*

PHOTO BY PROVIDED BY JONNI O'NEAL

Emerson knew both Hannifin brothers. Lawrence sold newspapers at the Idanha when he was a boy. He was known as the "toughest kid in Boise," said Emerson.

No one from the Hannifin family has owned the store since the late 1960s, but it kept its name, its old posters and its wood floor, worn as smooth as satin.

"Hannifin's has always been a direct line to the past," said historian Tully Gerlach. "How it was in the 1950s is the same as it was in the '90s — the 1890s and 1990s."

Even in the early days and despite the geographical isolation of the city, Boiseans kept up with national and international news. Places like Hannifin's that stocked periodicals from far-flung locales helped them do that, Gerlach said.

Through its many decades, the store attracted politicians, boxers, ditch diggers, wrestlers and Sen. William Borah. The potbellied stove that warmed the place is an icon in its own right — a fixture through the Jazz Age, the Great Depression, the World Wars, the Cold War, the Summer of Love and ever since. John Hannifin salvaged it from the Ada County Courthouse that preceded what's now considered the "old" courthouse on the Capitol Mall.

One mark of a place's iconic status may be the amount of folklore it fosters. Some insist Hannifin's basement is a portal to Boise's Chinese tunnels. The fact that historians have disproved the tunnels' existence means nothing in the face of urban legend.

Hannifin's is haunted, according to some. The ghost? He's a high-profile spirit: Raymond Snowden, aka "Idaho's Jack the Ripper," the last man hanged at the Old Pen.

Snowden stopped in at Hannifin's the night he killed a woman in Garden City in 1956. Someone found the knife used in the crime near the store.

Granddaughter O'Neal remembers visiting Hannifin's in the 1950s when she was a girl.

"There was this incredible smell when you came through the doors," she said. "And my grandfather had one of those old-fashioned Coke machines. You'd reach in, pull your bottle out and have the feeling the machine was going to capture your whole arm."

Hannifin kept his granddaughter stocked with a never-ending supply of comic books and empty cigar boxes from around the world.

For a little girl in the 1950s, Hannifin's was a thrilling and sometimes taboo place.

"I could only go past a certain point in the store," remembers O'Neal. The back of the store was for men only. Posters featuring Gibson girls and languid "cigar women" hung on the walls.

"Not what we would consider risque, but provocative for that era," said O'Neal.

Her grandfather habitually worked 12-hour days at his store. He walked home to his house in the North End for lunch, then walked back again — except when it snowed.

"He loved his work. He was a man in-the-know," said O'Neal. He always wore a suit to work, even during the summer when nothing but a small fan cooled the shop.

O'Neal and her grandchildren still like to visit.

"I can close my eyes and see my grandfather there. It's just joyous to see his name on the side of the building," she said.

Hotel Manitou 'Ghost Sign'

"Ghost sign" is the term for a hand-painted advertisement that has remained on a wall for so long, it's faded to the point of resembling a phantom.

The ghost sign on the side of the former, and long-vacant, Hotel Manitou on Main Street between 10th and 11th may be faded, but it's one of the most recognizable sights in Downtown Boise.

Like so much old advertising — cigarette ads from the 1940s that tout tobacco as a health and digestion aid come to mind — the wording is wonderful. The Manitou ghost sign offers what appears to read "strictly modern" rooms for 75 cents per day.

The Dec. 18, 1910, issue of the Idaho Statesman reported the news of the opening of the Hotel Manitou alongside brief items about a young woman searching for her missing brother, a call for Christmas dinners donated from the "housewives of the city," and a note that despite a recent frost, plums left unpicked had not fallen from the limbs of a small tree at 6th and Idaho.

The hotel was set to open Christmas Eve, according to the newspaper, "equipped with a well-lighted white marble entrance and a well-appointed lobby." The hotel had 38 rooms, "many equipped with private baths."

Noel Weber Sr. from Boise's Classic Design Studio says ghost signs like the Manitou have lasted so long because painters used white lead to mix their paint. They worked fast, said Weber, because they were usually paid by the square foot. They worked suspended by block and tackle (or ropes and pulleys) on bosun chairs like those window washers use today.

Among Boise's other notable ghost signs: the C.C. Anderson Department Store sign in the alley next to Red Feather on 8th Street. It boasts dry goods, millinery (hat making) and "etc." among its wares.

Another ghost sign with a massive, round target is still visible on the former bow and arrow shop just north of the Central Fire Station building at 6th and Idaho streets.

Downtown Boise also has a couple of antique advertising signs that look new again. Classic Design Studio restored the Eagles sign on the Jones Block at 6th and Idaho and the 1912-era Stearns car advertisement on the east wall of the Adelmann Building on Idaho Street at Capitol Boulevard.

PHOTO BY DARIN OSWALD

DID YOU KNOW?

"Manitou" is an Algonquin tribe word for a spirit of the natural world. Manitous can have both good and evil influences. Ghost signs attract fans who travel the U.S. and abroad to photograph them before they disappear. Groups such as the Society for Commercial Archaeology (sca-roadside.org) document antique signs as well as other aging roadside attractions, such as gas stations, amusement parks and hotels.

Idanha Hotel

The predecessor of the Boise Depot on the bench was a passenger depot built in 1894 at Front and 10th streets in Downtown Boise.

That building, say historians, opened the door for the construction of a first-class hotel. Boise architect William S. Campbell (whose firm became what is now CSHQA) designed the Idanha in 1900.

The origins of the word "Idanha" are hazy. By some accounts, it's a variation of a tribal word for healing waters. By other accounts, it's a made-up word. It was the name of a bottled water from Soda Springs that won a top prize at the Chicago World's Fair in 1893.

In any case, when the hotel opened its doors on New Year's Day, 1901, the Idaho Daily Statesman called it "the acme of perfection." The Idanha had one of the first elevators in the state and offered visitors amenities such as electric lights and telephones.

The Idanha's French chateau style is visible in its spires and turrets as well as its notched roofline.

The building is architecturally unusual in Boise. But beyond the bricks and mortar, it's also one of

DID YOU KNOW? *Just after the turn of the 20th century, the Idanha was considered the height of elegance. The intersection of 10th and Main was notable for having a turret on each corner. The Idanha and the Gem and Noble turrets are still standing on the north corners. The southern corners lost their turrets. One, from the W.E. Pierce Building, now stands in C.W. Moore Park with other architectural remnants.*

PHOTO BY DARIN OSWALD

the most storied buildings in the city. Presidents Theodore Roosevelt, William Howard Taft and Benjamin Harrison stayed there, as did actress Ethel Barrymore. According to several sources, singer Roger Miller composed the American classic "King of the Road" at the Idanha. (A public art piece by Marianne Konvalinka across from the hotel on 10th Street includes the song's musical score).

The hotel's most famous association may be with the "trial of the century" in 1907. The state of Idaho put union leader William "Big Bill" Haywood and two other union officers on trial for hiring Harry Orchard to assassinate former Idaho Gov. Frank Steunenberg. The governor had earned the wrath of unions by declaring martial law and calling in federal troops to stop a labor uprising in North Idaho in 1899. A jury acquitted Haywood, thanks, perhaps, to an 11-hour speech by celebrated defense attorney Clarence Darrow that moved women in the courtroom to tears.

Many of the people associated with the trial stayed at the Idanha, including prosecutor William Borah.

Frank Gooding, governor during the trial, feared for his own safety during that tense time. He and his family decamped from their mansion on Warm Springs and took up residence on the Idanha's third floor. Darrow found the Idanha oppressive and rented a small cottage near Warm Springs instead.

In later years, the hotel lost its grandeur and got a little threadbare. Still, celebrated musician Gene Harris led Tuesday night jam sessions in the hotel's lobby bar. Musician Curtis Stigers cut his jazz teeth there in the 1980s when he was just a teenager.

Anthony Lukas, author of "Big Trouble," the definitive book on the Haywood case, wrote the author's note for "Big Trouble" in 1996 in Idanha Suite 306. He called the hotel a "creaking relic of its former splendor." In those years, the Heaven on Earth Inns Corp., a subsidiary of Maharishi Mahesh Yogi's Transcendental Meditation Program, owned the hotel.

Today, Parklane Management Co. has converted the Idanha into apartments and businesses.

Hoff Building

The opening of the Hotel Boise in 1930 was notable for a few reasons.

Boise had two other grand hotels in its Downtown core at that time, The Idanha and The Owyhee, but they had been around since 1901 and 1910, respectively.

The Hotel Boise on 8th and Bannock was bigger. It was taller. Boiseans, including the group of local artists who laid the groundwork for what would become the Boise Art Museum, flocked to the hotel's swank Crystal Lounge.

In 1930, only the dome of the Idaho Capitol stood taller than the Hotel Boise. The hotel had 10 floors and an octagonal penthouse. A giant, two-sided Hotel Boise neon sign shone atop the octagon. Each of the sign's letters stood about 8 feet tall.

A group of local entrepreneurs hired architect Frank Hummel (brother of Fritz Hummel, who designed the Egyptian) to design the hotel. It opened just after the stock market crashed in 1929.

As historian Arthur Hart noted in one of his history columns in the Idaho Statesman, the Hotel Boise hosted a Thanksgiving dinner in 1934, the heart of the Great Depression. On the menu: a choice of turkey, steak, roast young goose or roast suckling pig with all the trimmings, dessert and music by a live orchestra. The bill: 75 cents.

One story related to the hotel reveals that Boise was not immune to racist attitudes of the time. According to the Idaho Human Rights Education Center, opera star Marian Anderson performed in Boise in 1940. Hotel Boise management

FROM THE COLLECTION OF MARK BALTES

denied her a room. She stayed at the Owyhee after agreeing to use the back entrance and remain in her room when she wasn't performing.

The hotel underwent big changes in the late 1970s, including the addition of a three-story glass crown.

The Hoff Co. bought the building, renamed it and began a major renovation to convert it to commercial use in 1976. The company sold the building just two years later. The new owners, EBCO Inc., hired the local company Planmakers to restore some of the Art Deco detail that had been lost through the years, including reinstalling the marquees, flagpoles, door pulls and light fixtures, and restoring the stonelike appearance of the interior walls. Next time you walk by, check out the original, geometrical decorative elements on the Hoff's exterior.

Idaho Building

Construction of the Idaho Building at 8th and Bannock in 1910 marked Boise's entrance into the skyscraper era, according to Preservation Idaho.

W.E. Pierce, a real estate man who founded the Bank of Star and the Boise and Interurban rail system, hired Chicago architect Henry John Schlacks to design the building. Schlacks apprenticed under Louis Sullivan, a key figure in the development of modern architecture.

The Idaho Building, which had its centennial in 2010, reflected an aspirational spirit at a time when Boise was thriving. The city's population tripled from 6,000 to 18,000 between 1900 and 1910.

Many of the notable features of the Idaho Building are still visible, including a high-ceilinged lobby

PHOTO BY JOE JASZEWSKI

DID YOU KNOW? *The Idaho Building is listed in the National Register of Historic Places.*

and arched entryway with crown moldings. Floors in the lobby and hallways are covered with small green and white hexagonal tiles. The baseboards in the hallways are marble. Double-hung sash windows and an old-style elevator remain.

The building opened its doors just

four years after the San Francisco earthquake and fire. An article in the Idaho Daily Statesman made much of the then-new Idaho Building's sturdy steel and cast iron construction. Heavy layers of fireproofing wrap its columns.

The Idaho Building fell out of style in the 1970s, but unlike many of its contemporaries, it escaped the wrecking ball.

The local company Parklane Management Co., headed by Ken Howell, converted the building to mixed-use in the 1990s. That includes apartments on the top floors.

Residents enjoy geothermal heat, a sense of stepping back in time and front doors with glass windows like something out of a film noir. At one point, a resident wrote "Sam Spade" on the cloudy glass of his front door, harking back to the fictional detective who would have felt at home on 8th Street.

Federal Building/ U.S. Post Office

This Beaux Arts building opened in 1904 as the federal courthouse and main post office. Beaux Arts style is characterized by a rusticated first story, a grand entrance and arched windows. The style was popular for public buildings in the late 19th and early 20th centuries.

The building has wrought-iron decoration over its doorways and a pronounced parapet near its roof. Its stairs are made of some of the largest blocks of stone ever quarried in the area.

An L-shaped addition on the building's north side in 1930 made room for more agencies. Eventually, though, the building's functions outgrew their space. The federal court relocated to Fort Street near the

PHOTO BY JOE JASZEWSKI

DID YOU KNOW? *When Idaho Public Television made the movie "Assassination: Idaho's Trial of the Century," about the Haywood trial and the assassination of Gov. Frank Steunenberg, filmmakers shot the courtroom scenes in the old federal building. The actual 1907 trial took place in the original Ada County Courthouse at 6th and Jefferson.*

Veterans Administration. The main post office moved to 13th Street.

Today, the building is home to the Borah Station Post Office. An imposing portrait of Sen. William Borah peers down on visitors in the lobby.

Inland Spire

Some have called the concrete spire in the corner of the Hoff Building's parking lot at 8th and Jefferson streets Boise's miniature skyscraper. Some have speculated that the 25-foot object is a model of the Empire State Building.

It's actually a remnant from the old Inland Coca-Cola Building Co. building that stood at 12th and Idaho streets.

In 1979, when the pop plant was being torn down to make way for a parking lot, forward-thinking Boiseans, including planner/design consultant John Bertram and Phil Murelaga, one of the Hoff Building owners, helped save the 5-ton spire.

A crane moved it to its present site, where it remains a piece of public art. Its Art Deco style — seen in its vertical lines, a sense of aerodynamics and geometry — is in harmony with its bigger cousin, the Hoff Building.

DID YOU KNOW? *You can still see holes near the top of the Coca-Cola spire that held rings of glowing neon.*

PHOTO BY ANNA WEBB

Lincoln on the Capitol Mall

Abraham Lincoln signed an act that created the Idaho Territory in 1863. Considering that longtime connection with the state, it's appropriate that a statue of Lincoln should have such a prominent spot at the heart of the city.

The statue's first home in Boise was on the grounds of the Old Soldiers Home. The Ladies of the Grand Army of the Republic, the organization for wives and relatives of Union soldiers, raised money to place it there in 1915. When the home was torn down in the 1970s to make way for Veterans Memorial State Park, the statue moved to the grounds of the Veterans Administration at Old Fort Boise. And when the VA expanded in 2009, the statue moved again — on the 200th anniversary of the president's birth in 1809 — to the Capitol Mall.

The pedestal features a plaque with the words of Lincoln's Gettysburg Address and an engraving of the last paragraph of his second inaugural address.

Also note the small marker not far from the statue's base. It's an old surveyor's benchmark, preserved in recognition of Lincoln's early vocation: land surveying.

DID YOU KNOW? *By one account, this is the oldest Lincoln statue in the West. Sculptor Alphonso Pelzer used the president's death mask as a model.*

IDAHO STATESMAN FILE

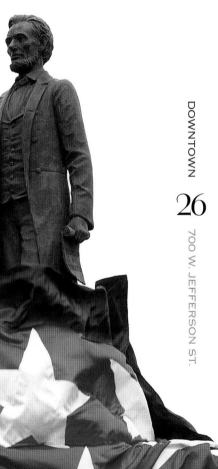

Idaho State Capitol

Though it's an icon that belongs to the entire state, the Capitol is the heart of Boise. Anybody can enjoy a singular pleasure whenever they feel like it — walking into the building through unlocked, unguarded doors. They frequently find they have the massive space to themselves. Despite its volume and its purpose, the Capitol has always seemed more light and warm than somber.

This might have something to do with the intentions of the building's architect, John Tourtellotte, who said, "The great white light of conscience must be allowed to shine and by its interior illumination make clear the path of duty."

Tourtellotte and partner Charles Hummel integrated light shafts, skylights and reflective marble inside the building to take advantage of Boise's copious natural light.

The white-domed building had a predecessor, a gabled, brick territorial Capitol built in 1886. It stood between Jefferson and State streets and 6th and 7th streets.

By 1905, Idaho had outgrown the territorial building. The Legislature approved construction of a new building. Tourtellotte and Hummel got the contract (around the same time they were building St. John's Cathedral on 8th Street). They built the dome and central parts of the Capitol first, between 1905 and 1912.

They finished the wings on the east and west sides in 1920. Demolition of the territorial building made way for the east wing.

The building underwent renovations in the 1950s and 1970s. A massive and fastidious two-year renovation between 2007 and 2009 added new subterranean wings and restored the building to its 1920 grandeur.

The renovation spared no detail. Craftspeople even replicated furniture and light fixtures in the styles of the originals. Workers kept notable features intact, including the 12 white lion heads in the Senate Caucus room; the treasurer's safe, as ornate and detailed as a giant Swiss watch; and the window casements made from wood taken from a Honduran forest at the turn of the 20th century.

Builders also removed dropped ceilings and reopened spaces as Tourtellotte and Hummel intended.

Among the most notable is Statuary Hall, a barrel-vaulted room that is among the most wonderful public spaces in the city. Have something on your mind? You won't find a better spot to sit and think things over.

Two statues stand nearby on the fourth floor: George Washington on horseback and the replica of "Winged Victory." Both are icons in their own right, included in this book.

The Capitol grounds offer up more special objects: statues of Gov. Frank Steunenberg and Abraham Lincoln, an Oregon Trail monument, and an 1840 cannon used by the Confederacy in the Civil War.

A model of the Liberty Bell, given to the state by the U.S. Treasury in 1950, adorns the Capitol's front plaza.

Ostner's George Washington

The statue is one of the oldest objects in the Idaho State Capitol. Its creator, a German immigrant named Charles Ostner, began carving the statue shortly after his arrival in Garden Valley in 1864.

Ostner had studied art at the University of Heidelberg and had become well-known as a sculptor in California before coming to Idaho. As legend has it, he carved the George Washington statue out of a single, massive block of Idaho pine.

A toll bridge operator by day, Ostner finished the statue at night by the light of candles and pine torches over the course of four years. He consulted a postage stamp for a likeness of the president. The finished piece was bronzed and installed on the territorial Capitol grounds in 1869. Damaged by weather, it moved inside in 1934. It got its coat of gold leaf in 1966.

Ostner continued his artistic career in the fine art realm, but also in the tabloid realm. In 1880, The National Police Gazette, a paper specializing in sensational murders, squalor and crimes of passion, published Ostner's sketch of the crime scene after a glamorous dance hall owner and her husband were murdered in the Idaho mining town of Bonanza.

Ostner fans take note: He carved a gold horse head that hangs on the second floor of the Idaho State Historical Museum, not far from DejaMoo, the stuffed two-headed calf, another Boise icon.

Ostner died in 1913. He is buried with his wife, Julia, in Boise's Morris Hill Cemetery.

PHOTO BY LINDSIE BERGEVIN

DID YOU KNOW? *The statue was repaired as part of the 2007-2009 Capitol remodel. It got a new base made from the salvaged wood of some of the historic Capitol grounds trees that were cut down during the Statehouse renovation.*

'Winged Victory'

The original "Winged Victory of Samothrace" is a second century B.C. marble sculpture of Nike, the Greek goddess of victory. Lost for centuries and rediscovered in 1863, it's on display at the Louvre Museum in Paris.

Idaho's own copy is on display on the fourth floor of the Idaho Capitol.

The statue arrived in Idaho in 1949 on the "Merci Train." After World War II, the people of France sent gifts to the capital cities in each state in the U.S. to thank Americans for the food, medicine, fuel and clothing aid they sent during the war.

The statue was one of several gifts. The boxcar itself was once on display at the Old Idaho Penitentiary. It included a stool carved by an 83-year-old blind man, a toddler's dress made of peach silk embroidered with a musical score, a flour sack printed with the motto "A friend in need, a friend indeed," and several other items.

PHOTO BY KATHERINE JONES

DID YOU KNOW? *The Nike went into storage, along with the Capitol's other iconic statue, the golden George Washington on horseback carved by Charles Ostner, during the building's renovation that began in 2007.*

Old Ada County Courthouse

Sometimes, one's affection for something is directly proportional to its vulnerability.

The old courthouse, vacated by the county in 2002, has stood despite proposals to demolish it for state office space. Community members and preservationists rallied to save it.

After more than a decade of uncertainty, the University of Idaho started working with the State Board of Education and the Idaho Supreme Court to renovate the courthouse as the Boise home of U of I's law school and the state's law library.

For many people, the building is a manifestation of resilience — not just for its escape from the wrecking ball, but for the era of American history it represents.

Built in 1939 from a Wayland and Fennell and Tourtellotte and

326—ADA COUNTY COURT HOUSE, BOISE, IDAHO

2B-H1155

FROM A PRIVATE COLLECTION

DID YOU KNOW? *Officials unveiled a new memorial to Idaho's fallen soldiers on the front lawn of the old courthouse on Sept. 11, 2010. The memorial lists the names of the men and women who have died in service since the 9/11 terror attacks.*

Hummel design, the courthouse was a New Deal project — part of President Franklin Roosevelt's plan to put Americans back to work during the Great Depression. It's one of seven county courthouses built in Idaho between 1936 and 1940 with the help of federal funds.

The building's imposing appearance was meant to communicate confidence that the U.S. would move through a difficult era and into better times, say historians.

Construction company Jordan-Wilcomb contracted workers for the project. Tim Wilcomb, company president, said the company still keeps remnants of the job — a security spotlight like the ones that shone on the courthouse roof, and the metal forms used to shape the concrete for the building's decorative spires. Old company records list workers' names and their pay: $1 an hour for carpenters, 50 cents an hour for other laborers.

Structurally, the old courthouse is unlike other buildings in Boise, where sandstone is so predominant.

A skin of white Indiana limestone covers its first four stories.

A rooftop jail boasts hardware made by the same company that made the hardware for Alcatraz.

The jail was unique, wrote historian Arthur Hart in his book, "Echoes from the Ada County Courthouse." It was mere floors away from the courtrooms where the prisoners were tried. The jail also had its Hollywood moment. Clint Eastwood shot his 1980 film "Bronco Billy" in Boise. He needed a jail setting, but the jail on Barrister Street was too modern for him. He liked the look of the jail in the old courthouse.

The building's most famous feature may be its 26 interior murals. They represent one of the largest collections of New Deal art in Idaho. Workers installed them in 1940. They were immediately controversial.

A group of California artists painted them after the Idaho artist

hired for the project dropped out. Many said that the landscapes they portray look more like California than Idaho's sagebrush steppe. One image of men preparing to hang an Indian man who is on his knees offends modern sensibilities, even though the image is part of a narrative detailing the evolution from frontier justice to courts of law. For a time, the courts placed a large flag in front of it.

The murals are rife with quirks and curiosities. One woman is painted with three arms. A stylized city skyline depicts none of the buildings that actually stood in Boise in 1939.

Still, even with their many flaws, the murals represent an era in city history that was more admirable than not. Like the rest of the project, they provided jobs. They've inspired conversation and strong opinions, and the chance to look honestly at the social mores of their time ever since.

Idaho's County Seals

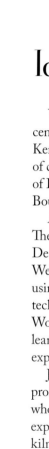
When Idaho celebrated its centennial in 1990, then-Mayor Dirk Kempthorne came up with the idea of creating decorative seals for each of Idaho's 44 counties to line Capitol Boulevard.

Albertsons sponsored the project. The Webers, owners of Classic Design Studio, got the job. Noel Weber Sr. proposed making the seals using a European porcelain enamel technique that became popular after World War II. Researching and learning the process took a year of experimentation, said Weber.

John Killmaster, a longtime art professor at Boise State University who knew the technique, lent his expertise. The Webers built a special kiln for the project.

Counties submitted design ideas for their seals.

After receiving a preponderance of gold miners, picks and shovels, the shop used a little creative license to come up with a varied mix of imagery.

The result is a series of unique seals on street lamps between Jefferson and Front streets. Each seal pays tribute to its county's special traits — a Weiser fiddler for Washington County, an Abe Lincoln hat levitating over a tractor for Lincoln County, an atom for Butte County, home to Atomic City, and so on.

DID YOU KNOW? *For the seals' unveiling in 1990, Boy Scouts made covers out of pillowcases. Boise Mayor Dirk Kempthorne drove up the boulevard in a Model T and revealed them one by one.*

PHOTO BY ANNA WEBB

Union Block

Like so many of Boise's architectural treasures, the Union Block, built in 1902, is made of local sandstone and brick. Its designer, John Tourtellotte, was one half of the firm Tourtellotte and Hummel.

The building's early investors (including Moses Alexander, elected governor in 1914) were sympathizers with the North in the post-Civil War years. As the story goes, they named their building the Union Block in keeping with their political allegiances.

Many businesses operated in the Union Block, including Boise Rubber Stamp and Pig, whose name is still barely visible on the building's alley side. "Pig" refers to pig iron. The company made metal block letters for printing.

Carlton's Dance Studio oper-

DID YOU KNOW?
The Union Block's former tenants have included, among others, Boise Mercantile, The OK Grocery, A.M. Beal's furniture store, Idaho Plumbing and Heating, and The Capital News Printing Co.

ated on the second floor in the space now occupied by the Rose Room. Many Boise women (and a few men brave enough to take ballet in the 1970s) will remember walking up the long staircase to Carlton's. That meant passing Whipple's gifts and luggage on the left, Fisher's office supply on the right.

Now-grown dance students might remember the dark paneling on the walls and the smells of hotplate meals that came through the walls of the single-room-occupancy apartments next door. The Union Block smelled of liver and onions.

In 1979, the building was listed in the National Register of Historic Places. But in the 1990s, it fell into disrepair and was in danger of being demolished. The city looked for someone to restore it. Boisean Ken Howell got the contract. Renewed, the building reopened in 1995.

Adelmann Building

Richard Adelmann, a German Civil War veteran, miner and businessman, fought in the battles of Antietam and Gettysburg. He moved to Boise in 1872 and opened a saloon on Main Street. Adelmann was a member of the city's volunteer fire department and staked a mining claim near Idaho City. In 1875, Adelmann married Emma Ostner, daughter of artist Charles Ostner, who carved the statue of George Washington at the Capitol.

Adelmann built his namesake structure in 1902. The Adelmann Building has housed many tenants, including a laundry and Stearns Motor Car Co. But for many Boiseans, the Adelmann is synonymous with its longtime resident, Fong's Tea Garden.

PHOTO BY DARIN OSWALD

DID YOU KNOW? *The Letterheads, a group of sign artists, painted this mural on the Adelmann's east wall in three days in 2000. The painting was based on an old advertisement for Stearns still visible on the building.*

The Chinese restaurant opened in 1937. Restaurateurs added the pagoda turret and Chinese character ornamentation on the building's corner. Fong's, known for its dark, bamboo-filled interior, operated for four decades. For this writer, walking to Fong's after the school day ended at East Junior High was a favorite trip. Waiters were old-school, no-nonsense. There was a small grotto near the restrooms. No one minded when a teenager was the sole afternoon customer and ordered only tea and an egg roll.

Property owners removed the Chinese characters on the celebrated turret in the 1990s.

Urban Peregrines

Peregrine falcons nesting on tall buildings are not unique to Boise. The nests and webcams that monitor them 24/7 exist in places as far-flung as Jersey City, N.J., and Kansas City, Mo. For a time, a pair of peregrines took up residence atop the sugar beet factory in Nampa.

But urban peregrines are, somehow, classic Boise birds. Like the Foothills, the Greenbelt and the Boise River, the birds represent yet another way that nature is woven into the unique life of this particular city.

For years, cameras have captured wild peregrines nesting in a box outside the 14th floor of One Capital Center at 10th and Main. The public has paid attention, tuning in to watch every nuance of avian drama. Viewers post a constant stream of updates: "Saw an adult peregrine preen,

April 30, 3:31:14 p.m. Saw an adult peregrine sleeping, April 30, 3:32:50 p.m." And so on.

In the city's sesquicentennial year, a peregrine pair at 10th and Main was caring for four eggs — an average number, according to biologists. The chicks, called eyases, leave their nests in early summer. They prepare by taking short test flights. Parents continue to feed them while they hone their flying and hunting skills. Thanks to webcams (sponsored by The Peregrine Fund, the Idaho Department of Fish and Game and Fiberpipe), residents have an up-close view every year.

The peregrine falcon represents a wildlife recovery success story. Peregrines had almost disappeared from Idaho by 1974. The Peregrine Fund began breeding and releasing

DID YOU KNOW? *"Falco peregrinus" is the scientific name of the peregrine falcon. "Peregrine" is Latin for wanderer. The birds often migrate long distances over the winter. Shown here: a screen shot taken in 2013 of the nesting box high above 10th and Main, with one of its residents.*

birds in Idaho and surrounding states in the 1980s. The federal government removed them from the endangered species list in 1999.

The U.S. Fish and Wildlife Service continues to monitor their numbers. The birds are fully protected under state and federal law.

Central Fire Station

Boise's first fire department consisted of 28 volunteers who began meeting in 1876 in an old blacksmith shop on Main Street. The shop had two stalls, one of which held the city's first fire engine, the Silsby steamer, which arrived in 1879.

The volunteer force remodeled the shop, adding a room for a watchman and a bell tower. In an undeniable twist of irony, the firehouse burned to the ground in 1883.

The department relocated to various Downtown homes until it landed at the corner of 6th and Idaho streets in 1903. The move to the new Central Fire Station also marked the end of the volunteer force. The city hired professional firefighters to protect the city.

The Boise Fire Department and Central. Fire Station.

DID YOU KNOW?

The brass pole that firefighters once used to get between floors remains.

FROM THE COLLECTION OF MARK BALTES

The two-story brick station had seven stalls for horses and equipment. Firefighters lived upstairs. The city bought a Metropolitan No. 3 steam pumper from the American Fire Engine Co. in 1903.

Other fire stations sprang up around the city in the decades that followed. By the 1980s, the department had outgrown Central Fire Station. The city built a new Station 1 on Reserve Street to replace it.

Central Fire Station and its 68-foot bell tower still stand on one of Downtown's most prominent corners. The building has a new life as a home to a restaurant and businesses. The station's bell hangs in the tower, on loan from its owner, the Idaho State Historical Society.

Flying M

"Forget about San Francisco, Portland or Seattle. Boise is the king of independent coffee shops," said Kurt Zwolfer.

The education specialist at The Idaho State Historical Museum nominated the Flying M, which opened in 1992, as a classic Boise icon. He loves the coffee, baristas who read his mind and one of the best people-watching spots in Boise.

Flying M's real fame may be its philanthropy. Original owners Lisa and Kevin Myers started the Valentines for AIDS silent auction 20 years ago. Hundreds of artists donate their work. Proceeds go to S.N.A.P., an organization that supports men and women living with AIDS and HIV.

Kent Collins bought the shop from the Myerses in 2011. He

PHOTO BY DARIN OSWALD

DID YOU KNOW? *Lisa and Kevin Myers opened a second Flying M in Nampa. They're still involved with the shop in Downtown Boise. Lisa helps with Valentines for AIDS. Kevin still roasts the coffee beans for both shops.*

continues the annual event. In its 20-year run, Valentines for AIDS has raised $373,765 for the cause.

Kirk Montgomery (who, with the Myerses, got the shop going those many years ago) shed some light on Flying M's name and logo. It comes from Kevin Myers' dad's cattle brand. Montgomery has it tattooed on his arm.

City Hall Fountain

This fountain once stood in front of Boise's original City Hall on the southeast corner of 8th and Idaho. You can make it out in old photos.

The Women's Christian Temperance Union gave the fountain to the city in 1910. The gift was part of the group's campaign against alcohol.

The WCTU installed what came to be called "temperance fountains" throughout Boise, mostly in front of saloons. The group had worked to enact "No Liquor Sundays" in Boise in 1902.

Few fountains of this type remain. Almost all were melted down during World War II so their metal could be used in the war effort. City historians believe this fountain survived because it had been painted. The paint camouflaged its materials.

Still, a rather surreal 1931 Statesman story titled "Inanimated Interviews" included a quote from the fountain itself:

"It took many ice cream socials to pay for me. I resent the gilt paint which is put on me from time to time under the direction of well-meaning but ill-advised city officials, for I am real bronze and would still be a beautiful thing if only some way could be found to get the paint off and permit me to be my natural self."

When the old City Hall was torn down in 1953, workers placed the fountain near the Statehouse. The fountain moved again in 1980 to its current location on City Hall Plaza. Several women who were present when the temperance union gave the fountain to the city in 1910 took part in the rededication.

The Boise chapter of the National

PHOTO BY ANNA WEBB

DID YOU KNOW? *A Mrs. W. S. Chipp, president of the local temperance union, had the honor of presenting the fountain to the city in 1910. She said, "The WCTU believes water to be the greatest necessity of life, it having been demonstrated that while one can be deprived of food for days, water must be had."*

Organization for Women stripped off the fountain's paint and renovated its plumbing.

IDAHO STATESMAN FILE

DID YOU KNOW? *Alison Sky's original design included cuts into the sidewalk below the sculpture that would echo the cuts of the granite above. That didn't prove practical for a busy street corner.*

'River Sculpture'

It's fair to say "River Sculpture" by New York artist Alison Sky is one of the most controversial pieces in Boise's public art collection. It was installed on the facade of The Grove Hotel in 1999. It's been a lightning rod for differing opinions ever since.

According to a plaque in the hotel lobby, Sky intended the piece to be a vertical river, paying homage to water, the "lifesource of Boise."

That idea is sound, considering the central role the river plays in Boise life. The city's underground roils with geothermal springs. Workers even had to reroute a subterranean canal to build the hotel.

Some love the sculpture, with its iridescent bubbles levitating up through a granite seam. Statesman reader Laurel McGuire nominated "River Sculpture" as an icon along with the view of the state Capitol and the Foothills.

For others, the promise of a good idea clearly has not delivered. "River Sculpture" has suffered vandalism. It's garnered its share of unfortunate nicknames through the years — "The Crack," among others.

In any case, the sculpture, which the Capital City Development Corp. donated to the city of Boise in 2003, is showing its age.

Its blue paint is chipped. A water feature that once created clouds of mist has been shut off since 2009. The city, the artist and the hotel have been working to "find a long-term solution" to renovate the sculpture, said Josh Olson of the city's Department of Arts and History.

Telephone Building

Thanks to Rocky Mountain Bell Telephone Co., Boiseans could make local telephone calls by 1884 and long-distance calls by 1899.

The growing company needed a Boise office for its workers and equipment. It bought land on Main Street near 6th.

Rocky Mountain Bell razed the existing building on the site, the law office of Territorial Secretary E.J. Curtis, and built the structure that stands today in 1899. William Campbell, who also designed the Idanha Hotel around the same time, was the architect.

The telephone company opened its doors on Jan. 1, 1900.

Operators ran switchboards on the second floor. Residents made their long-distance calls from special booths on the first floor. Telephone equipment, modern for its time, filled the basement.

Historian Arthur Hart called the building a "small gem in the Romanesque Revival style," with its thick walls, carved columns and massive, arched windows.

Note the rusticated sandstone used at the building's street level. The second story and pediment feature the same sandstone — but with a smooth finish. The building's facade is remarkably well preserved, even though it's more than a century old.

Look for the detail on the acanthus leaves that crown the columns. It's like the leaves were carved yesterday.

The word "telephone" is still etched into the building's facade.

PHOTO BY ANNA WEBB

DID YOU KNOW? *Hailey had the first telephone service in Idaho, established in 1883. Boise caught up the next year. At right: Telephone Building circa 1925. Note the John Jedlick Cigar Factory next door.*

PHOTO AT RIGHT PROVIDED BY THE IDAHO STATE HISTORICAL SOCIETY, 74-153-3

Egyptian Theatre

PHOTO BY JOE JASZEWSKI

DID YOU KNOW? *The theater opened for business in April 1927. "Don Juan" was the first movie screened. The original poster's tagline: "A super spectacle depicting the romantic adventures of the lord of all lovers!" The Idaho Statesman described the opening day excitement: "From 16 directions the crowd pressed in, crushing and milling — and the band kept playing. ... People caught in the human morass ... now and again developed a bit of hysteria."*

Boise entrepreneur Leo J. Falk and a group of business partners commissioned Frederick Hummel to create the theater in 1927. Its design was the result of the wave of Egyptomania that swept the world after the discovery of King Tut's tomb in 1922. Hummel apparently spent hours at the public library sketching hieroglyphics and other Egyptian figures. His choice of ceramic roof tiles was a nod to the Spanish revival style that was also popular at the time.

Through the decades, the Egyptian was known as the Fox and the Ada.

Boisean Earl Hardy bought the theater in 1977, saving it from the urban renewal wrecking ball with mere days to spare. His daughter, Kay Hardy, and the Hardy Foundation led the 1999 restoration that returned the theater to its 1927 splendor, down to the green glass fruits that dangle from its chandelier.

The theater's many charms include

its pipe organ. According to legend, a young Jimmy Stewart frequented the theater and played the organ when he was an Army Air Corps trainee at Gowen Field during World War II.

In the mid-1970s, when the theater's future was uncertain, Boise architect Ron Thurber led an effort to buy and restore the organ. His group, the Egyptian Foundation, showed the silent feature "Wings" at the Egyptian as a fundraiser in 1975. Businessman Joe Terteling lent his WWI-era Sopwith Camel to hang from a crane over the marquee. A photo ran on The Associated Press wire service.

Nearly all of the imagery in the theater is taken directly from historical sources, including the blue-gowned women who saunter across the proscenium. They're mourning ladies, copies from the Papyrus of Ani. That's a famous version of the Book of the Dead, the scrolls written

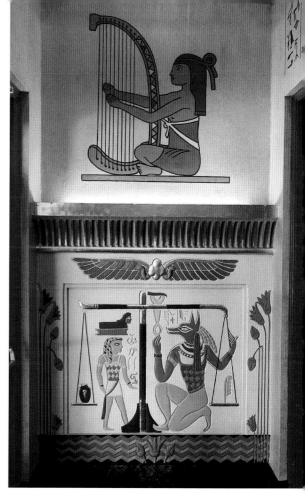

The theater's 1999 restoration included fastidious excavation of paint layers to determine the original color scheme.

IDAHO STATESMAN FILE

to guide ancient Egyptians through the afterlife.

There's fantasy in the Egyptian, too. The Statesman asked noted Egyptologist Stephen Harvey to "decipher" the theater's imagery in 2007. Harvey confirmed that the fanciful hieroglyphics throughout the theater's interior are just that — fanciful. It's the same story for the proscenium's gold swans. You would not have found gold swans in ancient Egypt, Harvey said. But you will find them at Grauman's Egyptian Theatre in Hollywood — one of the sites architect Hummel visited when forming his vision for Boise's beloved movie palace.

Today, the Egyptian hosts movies, concerts and lectures.

Pioneer Tent & Awning Building

The Pioneer Tent & Awning Co. operated for 70 years in Downtown Boise. Its sign, a white horse, still prances over 6th and Main.

Fourth-generation Boisean John Davidson nominated the building as a Boise icon. The company was still in business when he was a child.

"It was a magical place for a teenage boy. I'd go there simply to smell the smells. The aroma of leather and canvas greeted me at the door. They stocked tents and saddles, awnings, all kinds of camp gear. Tack for spirited steeds and trail-toughened mules were staples carried in bulk," wrote Davidson.

PHOTO BY DARIN OSWALD

DID YOU KNOW? *Pioneer Tent & Awning's white horse sign, an icon in its own right, dates to at least 1918. The city nearly lost it. After Pioneer Tent went out of business, the owners sold the horse at auction. It ended up at a local antique store. Longtime Boise store owner Hugh Angleton tracked it down. Angleton had it refurbished and returned to its proper place, where it remains today.*

Just walking into the store, he said, would sweep him "up to a high-mountain rendezvous, some grand jamboree out of A.B. Guthrie's 'The Big Sky.'"

The company was one of the first in the state to produce goods locally, rather than import them from the East, according to the Idaho State Historical Society. One of the company's founders, Ira Rohrer, helped start the business with a mere $11 in capital at the turn of the century.

In 1903, the company's ad in the city directory noted that Pioneer was a manufacturer and dealer in: "Tents, Awnings, Wagon covers, Machines, Hay and Grain Hauling, Miners' and Herders' Supplies, and Cotton Duck goods of every description."

Pioneer Tent operated out of a couple of different addresses on Main Street. The Pioneer Building we know today was built in 1910. By 1912, the company was the largest establishment of its kind in the state, with a staff of 20. It added a saddlery and harness-manufacturing operation.

The company evolved with the times.

By the 1920s and the advent of the automobile, the company was making more custom canvas tops for cars than wagon covers. Display and sales rooms filled the first floor. All the manufacturing happened upstairs.

Pioneer's traveling salesmen sold the company's wares beyond the Valley.

Boisean Patsy McGourty got her first job at the company in 1967. Pioneer was still making saddles and tents to order, she said. When customers paid for their goods, a pneumatic tube between departments zipped their money away. McGourty was on the other end and would zip a receipt back to them.

Every day at 3 p.m., she walked the day's receipts down to First Security Bank. The office manager timed her to make sure she didn't do too much window shopping along the way.

Pioneer stayed in business until 1971, still selling many of the same items it did at the turn of the century. It outlasted more than 7,000 competitors across the state, according to the historical society.

In 1974, Joan Davidson Carley, a descendant of Boise pioneer C.W. Moore, bought the Pioneer Tent & Awning building. Her renovations spurred new energy in the neighborhood.

The corner of 6th and Main is now one of the city's liveliest. The Pioneer Building, now filled with shops and restaurants, sits at the heart of the Old Boise Historic District, designated by the city in 1980.

Chinese Tunnels

Do honeycombs of Chinese tunnels lie beneath Boise? Historians say no. But ask any junior high kid, any lover of Boise folklore, any late-night denizen of Downtown, any conspiracy theorist, and you'll probably get a different answer.

Historians believe that the persistent urban tunnel legend had something to do with opium.

Large numbers of Chinese immigrants arrived in Idaho beginning in the 1860s. Some smoked opium. The Daily Statesman reported frequent police raids of opium dens throughout Boise's thriving Chinatown.

After the Idaho Legislature passed a law in 1881 "to prohibit the keeping of places of resort for smoking opium or frequenting same," opium dens moved underground — literally — into hidden basements around the neighborhood.

Historian Arthur Hart wrote that the occasional discovery of these dens in later years gave birth to the idea that Boise's underground was a vast network of chambers and passageways.

Historians and folklorists have investigated stories of underground tunnels across the western United States. Historians are unanimous in their belief that Chinese tunnels never existed in Boise, said Hart.

In the 1970s, when city leaders razed what remained of Boise's Chinatown, they found not a single tunnel.

Still, the story lives. Chinese tunnels are a Boise icon — if a fictional one.

"The lack of verification in no way diminishes the appeal that urban legends have for us," wrote Jan Harold Brunvand in his book, "The Vanishing Hitchhiker: American Urban Legends and Their Meanings." In Boise, the story of Chinese tunnels has hung on as strongly as stories of ghostly hitchhikers, Kentucky-fried rodents and beehive hairdos infested with spiders have hung on in other parts of the country.

Urban legends can arise out of societal beliefs and anxieties of a given era, Brunvand wrote. Chinese immigrants were no strangers to violent prejudice in Boise's early days. Tunnels fit a certain narrative of the Chinese as "the foreign 'other' burrowing beneath the streets engaging in nefarious activities," said Kurt Zwolfer, education specialist at the Idaho State Historical Museum.

As one story had it, Asian gangsters were known to pop up out of manholes, mug passers-by, then slip back down into the city's dark underground to escape forever.

On the other hand, one could say that the legend of Chinese tunnels persists because it has real allure in a world that can be all too explicit and illuminated.

Who hasn't passed a dark alley in Downtown Boise on a late night and hoped that one of those bricked-up walls was hiding something?

Who doesn't want to think that there's more to one's buttoned-up hometown than meets the eye? That goes a long way toward explaining the popularity of David Lynch movies.

Some years ago, the Statesman interviewed Alan Virta, then-archivist at Boise State University. We asked him what lost city relic he would most like to add to his collection. His answer: the secret map to the so-called Chinese tunnels.

"The tunnels are really a myth," said Virta, "but people contact us all the time about them. They want the maps. They want to believe."

DID YOU KNOW?

The few tunnels that do exist under Boise provide access to utility cables and the like. Pedestrian tunnels connect the Capitol to nearby state buildings.

Boise Christmas Lights

Idaho Statesman reader Erik Nystrom nominated the citywide Yuletide display as a Boise icon.

"It is so very cool and few cities 'do it up' like Boise," Nystrom said.

When the Downtown Boise Association formed in 1987, it took on the task of decorating the city for the holiday season, said DBA Executive Director Karen Sander. Decor has evolved from lighted wreaths to wrapping historic lampposts with lights and more. A grant paid for the arcs of lights with snowflakes that have appeared over Downtown intersections in recent years.

The DBA starts preparing for the light display the first or second week of November. That involves checking every bulb to make sure each one works, said Sander.

Boise's two public Christmas trees

— a city tree on The Grove, a state tree on the steps of the Capitol — also contribute to the annual show.

Boise has a long tradition of communal Christmas trees, dating to the 1860s. The nearest evergreens grew on the top of the Foothills. Most families didn't go to the expense and trouble to cut their own, according to city historians.

A note in the Dec. 19, 1871, Idaho Tri-Weekly Statesman concerns a public Christmas tree set up at the Good Templars Hall (6th and Main, where the Pioneer Building is today) "for the benefit of the children of Boise."

Residents were invited to "place articles on the tree" for their friends in preparation for a public party the night before Christmas Eve.

The U.S. Bank building's rooftop

DID YOU KNOW? *The state strung lights on the Capitol for the first time in winter 1912, shortly after the dome was built, in time for the January 1913 inauguration of Gov. John M. Haines. At right, the U.S. Bank building Christmas tree.*

PHOTOS BY DARIN OSWALD

Christmas tree is also a well-known icon.

The bank, built in 1978 and standing 267 feet tall, was the tallest building in Idaho for more than 30 years (the Zions Bank Building, now the tallest, topped out at 323 feet in 2013).

The U.S. Bank building has a permanent framework for its rooftop Christmas tree, said property manager Liz Fitzgerald.

Eight workers attach metal arcs to a retractable 12-foot "spine" every winter until the tree reaches a height of 85 feet. More than 3,500 LED lights illuminate it.

The structure is so high, the FAA requires building owner Unico to keep the tree lit all night so Life Flight pilots can see it clearly.

Weather determines when the tree comes down, said Fitzgerald. In a brutal winter, cables can freeze. Strong winds are dangerous for workers on ladders, so the tree stays up.

Sometimes, special circumstances keep the tree lit beyond the Yuletide season.

When Idaho hosted the 2009 Special Olympics World Winter Games, Unico kept the tree lit through the entire competition.

"People called it the Special Olympics party hat," said Fitzgerald.

Alexander Building

After Idaho Gov. Moses Alexander left office in 1919, he returned to his earlier vocation: merchant. He built the structure at 9th and Main in 1924 to house Alexander's men's store.

The public knew Alexander's as the "one price clothier." Unlike other stores, where customers bargained for the best deals, Alexander's marked its prices clearly. Bartering was not part of the shopping experience.

Alexander's is the only historic commercial building in Boise with a white terra cotta veneer facade. Its style is Italian Renaissance Revival. Traits include simplicity of design, classical elements such as columns, and the continuous "belt course" or strong horizontal band between stories.

The Second Renaissance style was

IDAHO STATESMAN FILE

DID YOU KNOW? *Fans of terra cotta ornamentation like that used on the Alexander Building, above, should look up a classic of the type: Louis Sullivan's Guaranty Building in Buffalo, N.Y.*

popular for courthouses, libraries and banks. This may say something about the gravitas with which Alexander approached his work. His name and initials still adorn the building.

Other remnants of Alexander remain in Boise. He bought three lots at the corner of 3rd and State streets in 1895. He hired local carpenters to build a Queen Anne-style house

based on pictures and floor plans they saw in the newspaper. One of his descendants sold the house to the state in 1977.

Alexander didn't leave politics entirely after leaving the governor's office. He served as a delegate to the 1920, 1924 and 1928 Democratic National Conventions. He died in 1932.

'Alley History'

Despite its somewhat secluded location, tucked into a Downtown alley on the north side of the McCarty Building, Kerry Moosman's ceramic mural "Alley History" consistently earns nods as one of the city's favorite pieces of public art.

Moosman, born and raised in Boise, installed the stoneware piece in 1992 after getting a grant from the city. The mural's imagery — Chinese calligraphy, advertising text, word fragments — is hyper-local, gleaned from Moosman's wanderings through his hometown, especially its back alleys. He made the piece as "a memorial to all that was lost," he said.

The Chinese text in "Alley History" is a nod to the writing that once adorned the turret of the Adelmann Building north of City Hall, not far from Boise's lost Chinatown. The mural's central spud king is an amalgam of Mr. Potato Head and the retro potato king decals that adorned many an Idaho kid's bike. Some say the fractured face resembles magnate J.R. Simplot.

"I never had that intention," Moosman said.

He wanted "Alley History" to harmonize with its gritty, urban site.

"When I was looking at the wall, I saw a pool of swirling cigarette butts under it. I knew that whatever image I put up would be reflected in that pool," said Moosman.

It took time for the city to embrace the piece. A Dumpster once stood in front of it. Vandals defaced it twice — once with whitewash, once with smeared body putty.

But "Alley History" survived. It

IDAHO STATESMAN FILE

DID YOU KNOW? *The mural includes a pair of shapely legs that reference '50s-'60s bombshell Jayne Mansfield.*

even set a visual tone for its part of the city. Freak Alley, the free-form outdoor art gallery celebrating street style, grew up around it.

Anduiza Fronton

The Anduiza family built their boarding house on Grove Street in 1914. The building offered something special: a fronton, or Basque handball court, in its basement.

The boarding house is long gone, but the fronton remains, essentially unchanged from a century ago. Boise native Mark Bieter, a blogger and co-author with his brother, John, of "An Enduring Legacy: The Story of Basques in Idaho," nominated the fronton as a Boise icon.

"If for no other reason, I think it deserves mention as one of very few century-old buildings in Downtown Boise that is still used for its original purpose," said Bieter, who researched the building for his Bieter Blog.

It's a big room, more than 100 feet long and 50 feet tall.

Dan Everhart from Preservation Idaho said the fronton building is one of the city's most notable historic structures, largely due to its rare combination of uses.

"Everything about that building was tied to the court. It wasn't like a boarding house with a court attached. It was more like a court with a boarding house attached," said Everhart.

Boise may have buildings that are more significant architecturally, but none is more unique than the fronton, Everhart said.

Frontons exist in other American Basque communities, including Elko, Nev.; Jordan Valley, Ore.; Mountain Home; and San Francisco. But the Anduiza is the oldest active fronton in the U.S.

Not long after the court was built, the Idaho Statesman reported "shouts and hurrahs coming from the vicinity of 6th and Grove streets," said Bieter.

He recalled a story told to him by an elderly Basque man. The "pelota," or ball used for handball, is hard like a baseball. Local players used to play until their hands swelled up. At that point, they'd enlist the help of boarding house owner "Big Jack" Anduiza, who would press their hands under a board, then stand on the board to reduce the swelling.

Bieter had the chance to meet Basque handball players who came through town. Shaking hands with them "was like shaking hands with a brick," he said.

Bieter remembers the fronton of the 1970s.

"It was a musty, dark place with lots of echoes. Shafts of light came through the few windows at the top and spread over the walls, on the hundreds of marks on the wall from all those balls over all the decades. You could hear pigeons in the beams."

The fronton had a rebirth as more American Basques traveled to Europe and learned Basque sports. An active group, the Boise Fronton Association, oversees organized leagues. They have spring and fall league play and tournaments in the winter and summer.

Bieter recalls speaking to a player from California. The player told Bieter that playing at the Boise fronton, hot, cramped and ancient as it is, was like a baseball player getting to play at Wrigley Field.

After the Anduiza era, an engineering firm occupied the fronton building for 50 years. Members of the Basque community bought it in the early 1990s. It's one of the buildings that form the heart of the Basque Block.

PHOTO BY JOE JASZEWSKI

DID YOU KNOW? *A pelota is a ball, but it is also a generic name for the games played in a fronton, said Mark Bieter. A pala is a wooden racket, as well as the name of a specific game. Above, Jason Crawforth plays at the The San Inazio Festival Pala tournament in 2008.*

Cyrus Jacobs/ Uberuaga House

Miners discovered gold in the Idaho City area in 1862. Pioneers platted the city of Boise in 1863. Cyrus and Mary Jacobs built their brick house on Grove Street (then called Market Street) in 1864.

The house is a centerpiece of the Basque Block. It's filled with historic objects and interpretive displays, and is open to visitors. It is the oldest brick dwelling in the city.

Cyrus Jacobs was a well-to-do merchant — the ultimate entrepreneur — who also served a term as mayor of Boise. He operated a variety of businesses. They included a flour mill, a soap factory, a meatpacking house and a distillery — the source of Jacobs' Best Rye Whiskey. He lived in his brick house for 40 years.

IDAHO STATESMAN FILE

In 1910, after the deaths of Cyrus and Mary, a series of Basque families lived in the house and began offering lodging for sheepherders. During this era, Boise's wealthiest families were leaving areas such as Grove Street and the nearby Central Addition neighborhood. They were relocating to newly fashionable spots such as Warm Springs Avenue.

The Uberuaga family began renting the home and operating their own boarding house in 1917. They bought the house in 1928 from the Jacobs' heirs and ran their business until 1969.

The house is one of the few remaining historic Basque boarding houses in the West. It has been part of the Basque Museum and Cultural Center since 1985.

The cultural center has overseen extensive renovations of the house, including reproducing wallpapers from the late 1800s. Restorers installed brewery-style light fixtures identical to those that hung in the house in the 1920s. Masons rebuilt three of five historic chimneys using old photos as their guides. Historic furniture fills the old house, including a dining room table built by boarders.

The historic house made the news in summer 2012 when University of Idaho archaeologists unearthed the contents of a newly discovered well. Some of the items recovered, which researchers believe date to the Jacobs family era, include a porcelain doll head; sarsaparilla bottles stamped with their place of origin: Lowell, Mass.; and an empty jar that once held "Oriental Tooth Paste," advertised as "England's Favorite Dentifrice," guaranteed to "impart a delicate fragrance to the breath."

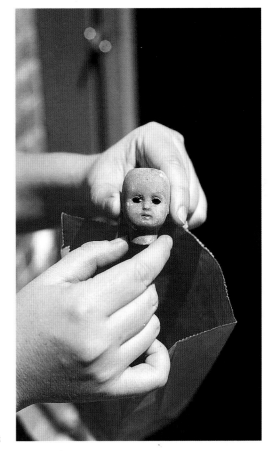

DID YOU KNOW? *About 1,000 people came to watch the 2012 excavation of the house's old well. The items uncovered will be used in archaeology lab courses at the University of Idaho. The community beyond Idaho also took note of the Boise dig. Later that year, Archaeology Magazine included it in the "World Roundup" of significant digs.*

IDAHO STATESMAN FILE

Trees of Gernika

In the 1980s, Boise's Basque community received three saplings from a famous oak in Gernika, Boise's sister city in the Basque Country in Spain. The ancient tree was a meeting place for Basque lawmakers through the centuries. It survived bombing during the Spanish Civil War and came to represent freedom, democracy and identity for the Basque people.

Officials and community members planted one of the saplings at the Idaho Statehouse. Vandals stole the sapling and replaced it with a twig.

Luckily, Idaho had two more saplings.

Pete Cenarrusa, Idaho's secretary of state at the time, planted one of them on the Statehouse grounds.

Basque President Jose Antonio Ardanza, making his first U.S. visit in 1988, planted the other seedling on the Basque Block in the front lawn of the Cyrus Jacobs/Uberuaga House.

Arborists relocated the Statehouse tree during the 2007-2009 Capitol renovation. It now grows near the southwest corner of 4th and Washington, just west of the Ruth Moon rose garden.

Boise resident Julian Achabal propagated seedlings from the tree on Grove Street. Achabal died in December 2011, but his trees —

DID YOU KNOW? *The symbolic oak in the Basque Country is actually a dynasty of four trees planted between the 14th century and 2004. The third tree is the tree that survived the bombing of Gernika in 1937 and provided the Boise saplings; it died in 2004. Gardeners replaced it with a descendant that grows today.*

PHOTO BY DARIN OSWALD

arboreal grandchildren of the tree in the Basque Country — are thriving.

One is at 6th and Grove in front of the Basque Museum. Another is growing at the Basque Cultural Center in Gooding.

American Cleaning Service Sign

Statesman reader Alan Harkness nominated the distinctive, rotating sign "that's been informing and entertaining us for generations."

The sign, at a prime viewing spot for commuters on Front Street, regularly features jokes and one-liners a la Reader's Digest.

Typical examples: "If wool shrinks when it gets wet, why don't sheep shrink in the rain?"; "A day without sunshine is like night"; and "If Jimmy cracked corn and no one cared, then why is there a song about him?"

Joe Schmoeger started posting jokes, as well as family milestones, on the sign after founding the company in 1949. His grandson, Eli Schmoeger, now runs the family business, which provides cleaning and janitorial services.

Eli has kept the sign tradition alive. These days, choosing quips is a group project. Employees and staffers pitch ideas.

"Everyone wants to be published," said Eli.

The community gets involved, too. People call to submit ideas for the sign. If the sign poses a question, chances are people will call or stop in to answer it, say staffers.

DID YOU KNOW? *American Cleaning Service opened its doors on March 15, 1949.*

PHOTO BY ANNA WEBB

Idaho Candy Co.

Before the refrigeration age, candy couldn't travel long distances. Regional sweets were a lot more common than they are now. A few remain in production, such as Valomilk from Kansas and GooGoo Clusters from the Deep South.

We have the Idaho Spud Bar — produced, as it has been since the end of World War I, on South 8th Street in Boise.

T.O. Smith, a journeyman candy maker, came to Idaho to help build the Dewey Palace Hotel in Nampa. Around 1901, Smith returned to his earlier profession. He started making candy and selling it door to door out of shoe boxes. Soon, he had a staff of 17 people churning candy out of a small shop near 8th and Fort streets in Boise.

In 1909, the company moved

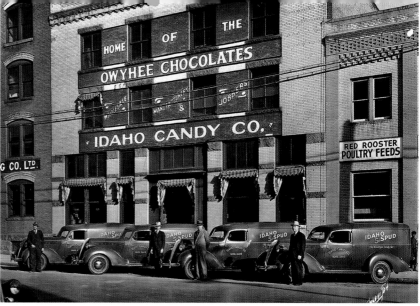

PHOTO PROVIDED BY IDAHO CANDY CO.

DID YOU KNOW? *The historic company introduced a new candy, Huckleberry Gems, in 2012. It was the first new bar in 50 years, said company owner Dave Wagers. A small shop at the factory often offers good deals on candy "seconds" that don't pass muster for commercial sale but are still delicious. Above: Idaho Candy Co. in the 1930s.*

to its present-day home. The 23,000-square-foot factory was among Boise's most modern buildings at the time. Boiseans considered it a progressive atmosphere for work-

ers because it had innovations such as skylights and a "welfare" room — break room — for employees.

Next time you walk by the building, look closely at its facade.

Each brick is individually painted in various shades of orange. Someone, said Dan Everhart of Preservation Idaho, then took the trouble to paint the mortar joints black.

Today, using some of the very equipment that was used in the early 1900s, the company makes a variety of candies, including Owyhee Butter Toffee, Burnt Peanuts, horehound drops and Chicken Bones — the latter an amalgam of molasses, peanut butter and coconut.

Three of its classic bars are still in production, including the Cherry Cocktail Bar (1926), the Old Faithful Bar (1925) and the celebrated Idaho Spud Bar, introduced in 1918. Despite rumors to the contrary, the Spud Bar does not contain potatoes. It resembles a potato, however, and has one of the most charming, retro-style wrapper designs around.

Many consider its slab of cocoa-flavored marshmallow covered in dark chocolate and coconut an acquired taste. The company originally marketed it as a health food, said current owner Dave Wagers, because it contains agar agar, a vegetarian gelatin made of seaweed. The company website features recipes for transforming the bar into a cocktail and into fondue.

The Idaho Candy Co. has produced more than 50 different candy bars over the years, including the Chicken Dinner Bar, the Big Chief, the Quarter Section and the Fox Trot. The product list from the years between 1919 and 1928 offers the perfect opportunity for a list poem:

"Boise Retro Sugar"

Owyhee Mystery Package, Owyhee Victorias, Owyhee Tasties, Owyhee Anticipation, Owyhee Package of Plenty, Owyhee Matinee, Owyhee Tete Tete, Owyhee Meditation, Owyhee Peg of My Heart, Owyhee Floradora, Big Eat Bar,

IDAHO STATESMAN FILE

DID YOU KNOW? *At one time, the Idaho Spud Bar was shaped even more like a potato. It had two rounded slabs adhered to one another by a chocolate wafer and chocolate syrup "glue."*

Hunky Dory, Kreamy KoKo Bar, Dainty Bits, Beetles, Bottles, Mice, Pipes, Slippers, Crabs, Hot Rolls, Dark Secrets, Brooms, Mapolette Society, Over the Top, Grasshopper Lunch, Midget Stix, Peter Pan, Roly Poly, Shimmy Dip, Sweet 16, Have-an-Egg, Tippecanoe, Fluffly Ruffles, Pecan Nut Tango, Uncle Sam Bar, Raspberry Jelly Cake, KoKo Paste, Daddy Paddles, Sweetheart Bar, Figgly Wiggly Bar, Poosey Bar and the Gin Fizz. The recipes are lost.

George's Cycles and Fitness

Joyce and Bob Sulanke arrived in Boise from Kansas some 40 years ago. Joyce was a national women's cycling champion. Bob was a math professor at Boise State.

The Sulankes opened the first incarnation of George's in 1971 in a shed behind their house near Warm Springs, said Mike Cooley, co-owner today with Tom Platt.

Joyce Sulanke named the shop after George Latham, owner of a celebrated bike shop in Lawrence, Kan., and creator of the motto: "Outfitters to the self-propelled."

The Sulankes' timing was good. They opened their shop just as the American bike boom was beginning, said Cooley. Ten-speeds were in big demand in Boise, arriving 400 at a time by train. The Sulankes kept spi-ral notebooks filled with the names of Boiseans waiting to buy bikes.

"They brought in brands that Boise had never seen, Peugeots, Gitanes. They created this niche market," said Cooley.

He remembers being a seventh-grader at North Junior High in 1971 and riding his Sears ten-speed out to the shed to see a bike that sold for $300.

"No one could believe there was a bike that cost that much," he said.

He bought his first set of toe clips at George's. He didn't know until later that Tom Platt was a young George's patron, too, saving his money for a European bike.

George's outgrew the shed in the mid-'70s, spending time in two different buildings on Broadway.

Cycling was booming, with a reputation for being somewhat eso-teric, a European pastime associated with the Tour de France and Italian black-and-white cinema. Mountain biking hadn't been invented yet.

Around 1979, cyclist Greg LeMond became the first American to race successfully in Europe. The seminal movie "Breaking Away" helped plant bike racing firmly in American popular culture.

George's thrived. The shop founded a home team that began competing throughout the North-west.

This writer's memory, circa 1980: walking home from a party late at night, hearing that distinctive click/hiss of bike wheels, turning to see a pack of young Boise men, clad in

George's jerseys, calling out "Buongiorno!" as they sped past under the streetlights.

Cycling wasn't just European anymore. Or if it was, it was European in a way that Boise liked.

In 1981, Cooley and Platt, both members of the George's racing team, bought the shop from the Sulankes. It has since grown into three shops and a bike-fitting studio.

George's is responsible for events that have become iconic in their own right. Bob Sulanke organized the first Bogus Basin Hill Climb in 1972.

"We kept the tradition going," said Cooley.

In 1987, George's organized the first Twilight Criterium, which draws racers from across the country.

IDAHO STATESMAN FILE

DID YOU KNOW? *The riders sponsored by George's, like this one training on North Cartwright Road in 2007, were among the first in the Treasure Valley to realize that the road to Bogus Basin was a great, and daunting, training road for cyclists.*

Belgravia Building

The Belgravia, built in 1904, was one of the city's first apartment buildings and, for a time, one of its toniest addresses. The Romanesque-style Belgravia originally had room for around 15 families. Later subdivisions of the building added more units.

Its original construction cost, $70,000, was a bargain considering the building has stood for more than a century with most of its original materials, doors and light fixtures intact.

Its locally quarried sandstone walls are thick — 2 feet at the basement level, decreasing to 18 inches at roof height. The roof is galvanized iron, both fireproof and soundproof. Some of the Belgravia's original

PHOTO BY DARIN OSWALD

DID YOU KNOW? *The Belgravia was renovated in 1977. Today it's home to several businesses. It won one of Preservation Idaho's first Orchid awards. That year it shared the honor with Old Boise, the Sonna Building, the Bouquet Bar and the Grand Army of the Republic Hall north of the Capitol.*

inhabitants enjoyed upscale amenities such as hot water and indoor plumb-

ing. No wonder some called the Belgravia "the castle."

Central Addition

This old neighborhood sits just north of Julia Davis Park, caught in a half-residential, half-commercial limbo in a rapidly urbanizing part of the city.

Preservation Idaho has had Central Addition in its sights as a "threatened neighborhood" for many years.

The centerpiece of the neighborhood is the Fowler House at 413 S. 5th St. Once one of Boise's finest houses, it sits boarded up and vacant. Its owner, a development company that owns other houses on the block, offered the house for free to anyone who would pay to move it. So far, no one has taken the company up on its offer.

Preservationists say the old neighborhood, platted in 1890, matters because it was one of the

PHOTO BY KATHERINE JONES

DID YOU KNOW? *The neighborhood's decline at the turn of the century was rapid. Union Pacific laid track on Front Street in 1903. The Central Addition became a less fashionable place to live as Warm Springs Avenue continued to gain prominence as the city's address of choice.*

first subdivisions outside of Boise's original townsite. And it was grand for a time, home to merchants, a Supreme Court justice, a secretary of state, a U.S. marshal and others.

Central Addition was quiet and elegant, surrounded by fruit orchards. Walk around the neighborhood and you'll still see traces of the grandeur that once was.

C. W. Moore Park

Affection for C.W. Moore Park is a complicated thing. On one hand, the park is a lovely place. Like the best urban "pocket parks," it offers a sense of cozy seclusion. There's even a little stream of running water.

On the other hand, the site is a reminder of Boise's lost buildings that fell during the urban renewal wave in the 1970s.

Remnants from old buildings on the site include the turret from the Pierce Building, built in 1903. It stood across Main Street from the Idanha Hotel. Demolition of the Pierce in 1975 made way for One Capital Center.

A stone from Central School occupies a central spot in the park. The school stood near the Capitol Mall. It was torn down in 1973.

The park's water wheel came from Morris Hill Cemetery. Similar wheels once dotted the city's extensive irrigation ditch system. The old Grove Street ditch, built in 1866 just three years after the city was platted, still runs along the south side of the park.

C.W. Moore, one of Boise's earliest residents and co-founder of the First National Bank of Idaho, gave the land to the city in 1916, the year he died.

He intended it as a children's park and playground. That finally happened a decade later.

Boisean Robert Barbour lived across the street from the park in a one-bedroom house with a sleeping porch until 1930, when he was 6 years old.

"I can still picture the park. I remember that it had swings, a slide and a large sandbox. As I recall, there were several large trees," said Barbour.

When he was a boy, 5th Street was unpaved and covered with sand, he said. He had another connection to the park and its generous donor. His father worked for many years at the bank Moore founded.

In 1956, a World War II barracks was moved to the site, displacing the playground. The building became the offices of the Idaho Society of Crippled Children and Adults.

When the society moved in 1975, the Boise Jaycees used the building as a community and youth center.

The building was eventually removed. The land returned to its intended purpose.

The city dedicated it as a park in 1983.

DID YOU KNOW? *Tiny as it is at .28 of an acre, C.W. Moore Park is not the city's smallest park. That honor goes to West More-land Park on the West Bench. It's just .26 of an acre. Pictured here in C.W. Moore Park is the entrance arch of the Bush Building that stood at Capitol Boulevard and Idaho Street, the current site of Boise City Hall.*

Old Assay Office

The discovery of gold led to the creation of the Idaho Territory in 1863. Between 1861 and 1866, the territory's gold output represented about 19 percent of the nation's total.

Shipping Idaho gold to the U.S. Mint in San Francisco was pricey, so in 1869, Congress approved $75,000 to build a U.S. Assay Office in Boise. Here, miners could have their gold and other minerals, including silver and lead, "assayed" for value.

Construction began in the summer of 1870 and took about a year.

The building contained heavy equipment, offices and a laboratory. It had a domestic side as well. The chief assayer and his family lived in an apartment on the top floor. Security guards lived in the basement. The building's style is Italianate, seen in its low-pitched roof, big eaves, modi-fied tower and square floor plan.

Between 1872 and 1933, millions of dollars in gold and minerals — by one account more than $1.5 million a year — came through the Assay Office's doors. The windows have security bars. The native sandstone walls are 2 feet thick.

The office operated until 1933, when the building became the headquarters for the Boise and Payette National Forests. The grounds became a public park. Most of the large trees growing there are more than a century old.

The U.S. Forest Service remodeled the building's interior in the 1930s, but its exterior is virtually unchanged since the year it opened. Historians regard it as one of the most significant examples of territorial architecture in the state. It is one of just 10 National

IDAHO STATESMAN FILE

DID YOU KNOW? *The Assay Office shares its neighborhood with other notable sites. One is the house at 140 W. Main St. (shown on page 254). Idaho Gov. James Brady lived there while he served, 1909-10. Behind the house is the Ormsby Stable, circa 1890. It boasts an oak stairway and bird's-eye maple doors. Lucky horses.*

Landmarks in Idaho, an honor shared with the likes of Cataldo Mission, the Lolo Trail and Experimental Breeder Reactor No. 1 in Arco. The building now houses the state's Historic Preservation Office.

Pittenger Sequoia

The massive sequoia (Sequoiadendron giganiteum) grows next to St. Luke's Regional Medical Center's Human Resources office on land that was once the estate of Alice and Fred Pittenger. Both Pittengers were doctors. Fred served as Idaho surgeon general. Alice became a champion of the Girl Scouts; a camp at Payette Lake still bears her name.

The tree began its Boise life as a cutting given to the Pittengers by forester and conservationist Emil Grandjean. The Pittengers' British gardener planted the cutting in 1912. It grew, even as Boise changed around it and the hospital campus expanded.

Alice died in 1953. Fred died in 1964. New owners moved the house to Caldwell. The sequoia remained.

St. Luke's began decorating the tree for Christmas in the 1980s. The tree began to deteriorate, dying back and dropping its needles. Experts determined that the decorations were doing the damage. St. Luke's stopped the holiday tradition. Hospital administrators called in a tree expert from California — native sequoia terrain — who recommended cutting 11 feet off the top of the tree to revive it.

The strategy worked. Arborists trained a "leader" branch toward the sky to replace the lost section. The result: a healthy tree with a shape resembling a Prussian helmet — or, better yet, the Idaho State Capitol dome.

The Idaho Big Tree program, a division of a national program that catalogues the largest trees in the U.S., has recognized the sequoia at St. Luke's as the largest of its species in the state. It stands 89 feet tall.

PHOTO BY ANNA WEBB

DID YOU KNOW? *The Pittenger tree, pictured here, has a cousin: an impressive sequoia on the grounds of North Junior High at Fort and 13th streets.*

Chapter Two   SOUTH BOISE/THE BENCH

Julia Davis Park

Tom Davis left his home in Cincinnati in 1862 and traveled west. Like so many other prospectors, he hoped to strike gold. Instead, he settled in the Treasure Valley. He was among the pioneers who platted Boise's original 10 blocks.

By 1863, Davis owned large expanses of land between Grove Street and the Boise River. He grew produce and sold it to miners. By one account, he planted 7,000 apple trees along the river.

Tom married Julia McCrumb in 1871. Her bronze likeness stands in the park today. She was known for helping travelers as they made their way through Boise on the Oregon Trail. That generosity may have led to her death in 1907 after nursing a traveler with typhoid fever.

Tom Davis deeded 40 acres to the city in her memory. He stipulated that the city had to use the land as a public park. Davis himself died a year later.

Boise embraced its first park, which today covers nearly 90 acres in the heart of the city.

Diane Davis Myklegard, a great-granddaughter of Tom and Julia, organized the Julia Davis Second Century coalition to celebrate the park's centennial in 2007.

An outgrowth of that group has led efforts since to renovate and enhance the park. Julia Davis has a new agricultural pavilion not far from Zoo Boise. Projects in the city's sesquicentennial year included a Rotary Grand Plaza and an area dedicated to cancer survivors near the pond in the east end of the park.

Each of the park's iconic features

has a story.

The pond — now lined with willows, filled with murk and leisurely water fowl — was a deep and dangerous gravel pit in the 1930s. Winters were colder then. When the water in the pit froze, Boiseans skated. After a boy fell through the ice and drowned, city officials filled the pit to make it the shallow, lagoonlike body it is today.

The park's celebrated rose garden has interesting origins as well. According to city historians, Boisean H.C. Schuppel, chairman of a local men's garden club called the Cut Worms, got the idea for the garden in 1935. The club had two rules: no

DID YOU KNOW? *The Boise City Mounted Police disbanded in 2005. During the years they operated, their steeds lived in the stables on the park's north side.*

PHOTO BY KATHERINE JONES

women and no publicity. Fortunately, things changed. The garden received "public rose garden" accreditation in 1992. About 2,400 rose plants grow there today.

Many who grew up in Boise will recall that Julia Davis Park had its own amusement park. The "Fun Spot" offered a Tilt-A-Whirl that was terrifying for anyone of elementary age and a roller coaster with at least one stomach-churning curve.

The city built the California Mission-style band shell in 1928, which makes it just a few years younger than the Mission-style Boise Depot up the hill. The band shell provided a haven for folk singer Pete Seeger in 1968.

Seeger was scheduled to perform at Boise Junior College. College officials decided his left-leaning politics were too controversial. Seeger performed at the band shell instead.

The city dedicated the band shell to local jazz musician Gene Harris, who was a frequent performer there.

Chinese Temple and Herb Shop

Thousands of Chinese immigrants arrived in Idaho beginning in the 1860s to work in the mines and agriculture, and later on the railroads. Boise had a thriving Chinatown in the area loosely bordered by 9th, Idaho and Grove streets, and Capitol Boulevard. By the 1960s, many of the city's Chinese-Americans had moved away. In the 1970s, urban renewal swept away what was left of their buildings.

The Idaho State Historical Museum's exhibits of a Chinese temple and herb shop give a hint of this substantial part of Boise's ethnic past.

Opened in May 1972, the exhibits — down to the orange wax apricots in the blue and white porcelain bowl — haven't changed much in 40 years, said Rachelle Littau, curatorial registrar at the museum.

The herb shop exhibit is a re-creation of the Downtown shop kept by Dr. Ah Fong, then by his son and then by his grandson. Fong began his practice in Boise around 1890. His grandson, Gerald, practiced medicine in Boise until the mid-1960s.

Before it demolished what was left of Boise's Chinatown as part of urban renewal in 1971, the Boise Redevelopment Agency allowed museum staffers to go into the long-vacated Fong building on Capitol Boulevard to salvage items. Worn wooden drawers, the front window of the shop, medicine jars and other pieces of his shop are what museum visitors see today.

In addition to the items on display, the museum keeps a massive collection of Chinese herbal medicine from the Fong family. Scholars still seek

out the Boise collection for research, said Littau.

The temple artifacts have different origins. The Idaho Statesman ran an article in the early 1970s about the museum's plans to create an exhibit about Boise's Chinese population, said Littau, and Boiseans began donating art and artifacts.

It's likely the carvings and other items in the temple exhibit came from various locations around town, including a temple that stood on Front Street (torn down in 1937) and the Chinese Masonic Lodge that stood on Idaho Street near Capitol Boulevard (torn down during the 1970s).

A researcher, Chuimei Ho, visited Boise a couple of years ago to see the museum's opium-related artifacts. Littau asked her to interpret the large, gold carved panel, pictured at right,

that hangs as the centerpiece of the temple exhibit. Ho said the carving was made around 1906 by a Chinese company that supplied religious carvings to American Chinese.

It tells two stories. The top section portrays Xuan-mu, a female deity. The lower panel is an episode of a popular drama, said Ho. It features two sons of a prominent family showing their willingness to be deployed to battle.

Two donors gave the separate sections to the museum independent of each other.

"When we received them in the early '70s, historian Arthur Hart noticed that they fit together. We have no idea when they became separated from each other, but it's nice to have them reunited," said Littau.

PHOTO BY DARIN OSWALD

DID YOU KNOW? *The temple exhibit includes a collection of relics from Boise's Chinatown. A railing in front of the exhibit came from the balcony of the Hip Sing building. The Hip Sing was a "tong," or meeting house, that stood between Front and Grove streets where the Grove Hotel is now. It was demolished in 1972.*

Brunswick Bars

Before urban renewal swept through Downtown Boise in the 1960s and '70s, the stretch of Main Street from Capitol to 9th was home to more than a few taverns.

That stretch of streetscape was pretty lively. Besides the bars, there were movie theaters, pawn shops and loan sharks, said historian Tully Gerlach.

The vitality of Boise's Downtown modern street life, in evidence when you stroll 8th Street on a summer night or try to get a table at the newest brewpub, has more in common with the Boise of 100 years ago than it does with the Boise of 40 years ago, said Gerlach.

Old-style wooden back bars made by the celebrated Brunswick company — originally a maker of carriages and billiards tables founded in Ohio in 1845 — anchored some of the old Boise taverns. Owners would order the bars out of catalogs. Companies like Brunswick would ship them west in pieces for owners to assemble.

A few of the back bars are still around. The Brunswick at Pengilly's is a century old. It has company — an ancient National brand cash register.

The Bouquet has been in three different locations in Downtown Boise, said current owner Nathan Gorringe. The circa-1902 Brunswick bar has moved along with it, he said. These days, at its Main Street home, the Brunswick sits under a distinctive 1930s-era ceiling.

One of the most spectacular Brunswick bars in Boise is now at the Idaho State Historical Museum. Its owner was Madison C. Smith, described in the 1902-03 Boise City Directory as a "capitalist" with rooms at Main and 7th.

Smith's Brunswick bar dates to about 1880. Like the Brunswick at the Bouquet, Smith's bar moved around town. Drinkers enjoyed it at various Downtown locations for more than 70 years, according to the museum.

DID YOU KNOW? *Bars made by the Brunswick company became so popular just before the turn of the 20th century that the company opened a new factory in Iowa in the 1880s and began exporting wooden bars around the world. Pictured here: Smith's bar at the Idaho State Historical Museum.*

PHOTO BY JOE JASZEWSKI

DejaMoo

Few things in life are certain. This is: If you grow up in Boise and go on school field trips, you will encounter the stuffed two-headed calf at the Idaho State Historical Museum. And you will love him.

The creature, subject of a 2007 naming contest that christened him DejaMoo, was born on the Bemrose family farm in Gooding in 1950. He lived a couple of days. His legend has lived for more than six decades.

The museum made him into a plush toy around the time he got his name. A book near the museum's entrance is filled with photographs that travelers have sent back to Boise — plush DejaMoo at Monticello, at the Berlin Wall and at the ruins of Pompeii.

One photo, autographed by the deputy prime minister of China, features DejaMoo hovering over the skyline of Singapore. The Bemrose family gave the museum a photo, also in the book, of DejaMoo when he was still alive.

The birth of two-headed calves, while notable, isn't as rare as DejaMoo's celebrity suggests. Kim Taylor, museum store and visitor-services manager, said tourists have told her about similar stuffed calves in museums across the U.S.

But DejaMoo will always be a city treasure. The plush toy is a big seller for the museum.

"Even more for adults than for kids," said museum receptionist Maria Shimel. "He's definitely our mascot."

At the museum's 2012 Dia de los Muertos exhibition, DejaMoo was the centerpiece of a shrine devoted to lost pets.

IDAHO STATESMAN FILE

DID YOU KNOW? *E.H. McNichols, a taxidermist who lived in Star, preserved DejaMoo for the ages. The calf has become a de facto "him," but the museum doesn't have a record of whether DejaMoo was male or female. The taxidermy process removed any trace of telling anatomy.*

The Flicks

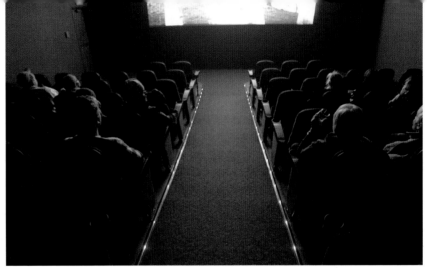

Photo by Darin Oswald

When The Flicks opened with a single screen in 1984, the closest things Boise had to "art house" cinema were occasional midnight screenings of "Woodstock" or "The Rocky Horror Picture Show."

The Flicks' double feature on opening night, "Casablanca" and "The Return of Martin Guerre," set the tone for the kinds of movies film lovers could expect.

"An American classic and a foreign art film," said owner Carole Skinner.

The theater's beginnings are grass-roots. Back in the 1980s, Carole's husband, Rick Skinner, belonged to "Films that don't come to Boise," a local club of cinephiles. Members invested in a 16 mm projector, rented space at the Y or the synagogue, and screened movies such as "My Dinner

DID YOU KNOW? *A staff of 36 volunteers takes tickets in exchange for free movies. It's one of the hottest volunteer jobs in town. There's a waiting list.*

with Andre" and "Diva." The club grew into The Flicks.

The theater lost money for its first seven years, but Boiseans eventually caught on.

Today, the community knows The Flicks for its movies, but also its outreach and benefit screenings for a diverse group of local nonprofits.

Boise resident Wally Smith nominated the theater as an icon.

"The Flicks is a community of staff, volunteers and patrons who enjoy Carole Skinner's out-of-the-mainstream, but prize-winning selections from film festivals we'd never otherwise see on a big screen," he said.

Boise Art Museum

It was the middle of the Great Depression. A group of forward-minded Boiseans seized the moment anyway to tend to the city's cultural life.

A group of 30 residents led by Cornelia Hart Farrer, Laura Moore Cunningham and others began meeting to talk about art. Their meeting spot: the Crystal Lounge at what was then the new Hotel Boise, known today as the Hoff Building.

Many were artists themselves who wanted an exhibition space. They founded the Boise Art Association in 1931. The group held the city's first formal art exhibition soon after.

Boise writer Rita Branham Rodriguez, author of "The Blue Doorknob: the Artistic Life of Cornelia Hart Farrer," said the show took place in

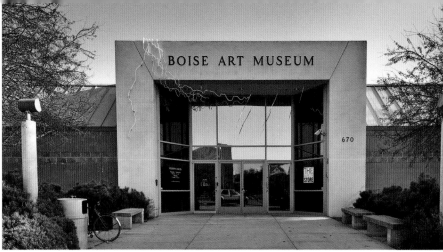

PHOTO BY DARIN OSWALD

DID YOU KNOW? *The museum's original Works Progress Administration-built facade and other walls are still visible, though the museum has expanded and modernized around them. The original facade forms the east wall of the museum's interior atrium.*

the former Idaho First National Bank building on Main Street. True to their grass roots, members of the group scrubbed down the walls themselves.

The group eventually partnered with the city and the Works Progress Administration to build the museum in Julia Davis Park on land given by the city. The museum, then known

as the Boise Gallery of Art, opened in 1937.

Farrer, who lived until 1991, kept close ties with the museum for the rest of her life.

She was a founder of the first Art in the Park event in the mid-1950s. Now one of the museum's signature events, it began modestly as an option for local artists who didn't make it into the annual Idaho Artist Exhibit. Artists hung their pieces on clotheslines strung on trees.

Like other Boise institutions, such as Bogus Basin, the Boise Art Museum is homegrown to its core.

Volunteers kept the museum running during its first three decades. The museum hired its first professional staff in the mid-1960s. It began to develop its permanent collection in the decades that followed. Works by the celebrated Idaho artist James Castle were among the museum's early acquisitions, said curator Sandy Harthorn. The museum's collection of Castle's art is one of the largest in the world.

Fred Pittenger, a well-known Boise doctor whose sequoia tree (another Boise icon) still grows on the grounds of St. Luke's, was one of the museum's first donors. He gave his collection of Asian works,

Portland artist Mike Rathbun and crew hoist a 57-foot diameter wooden ellipse into place in the museum's sculpture court in June 2011 for the exhibition "The Situation He Found Himself In." Rathbun designed the piece for the space.
PHOTO BY KATHERINE JONES

including several netsukes, or carved figures, in the 1960s.

BAM developed an education program for the public and underwent building expansions in 1973, in 1988 (when it became Boise Art Museum) and in 1998.

The museum collection includes 3,500 works, said Harthorn. It has a growing collection of 350 ceramic items, begun with a donation of

166 works from former Boise State professor and artist John Takahara.

Many of BAM's pieces have become iconic in their own right. Those include Deborah Butterfield's steel horse sculpture, "Democrat," named for one of her own horses, and the large enamel mural, "The Bright Land," made in the 1970s by John Killmaster. It hangs on the building's exterior.

Idaho Black History Museum

The museum began its life as St. Paul Baptist Church in 1921. Its original location was on the north end of Broadway Avenue (near Dona Larsen Park) on a piece of property donated to the congregation.

The church's first pastor, William Riley Hardy, was a skilled carpenter. He and his father-in-law, Louis Stokes, the church trustee, built the white clapboard structure themselves. According to museum literature, it is one of the oldest buildings in Idaho built by African-Americans.

World War II and the opening of Mountain Home Air Force Base brought more black families to Idaho. St. Paul's congregation grew. When it moved to a larger church in the early 1990s, it donated the old church for

PHOTO BY KATHERINE JONES

DID YOU KNOW? *Though it was built in the 1920s, a time when Mission-style architecture was popular, the church is colonial style. Its original windows are made with stunning earth, sea green and indigo tones. The congregation ordered them from a Sears Roebuck catalog.*

use as a museum. The Idaho Black History Museum was established in 1995. The old church was moved to Julia Davis Park and became the organization's home in 1998.

Today, the museum hosts exhibitions, events and community outreach projects.

Artist Faith Ringold immortalized the building after a 2008 visit to Boise. See her charming representation of the church, captured on a sunny Sunday morning, during your next visit to the museum.

Bob Gibb Friendship Bridge

PHOTO BY PETE ZIMOWSKY

Boiseans love their river. One of the city's best four-season spots to appreciate the beauty of that river — not to mention its cottonwood-lined banks, the Foothills beyond and a big dome of western sky — is the Bob Gibb Friendship Bridge.

City and university leaders started talking about building a bridge between the campus and Julia Davis Park as early as 1970. It finally happened in 1977, thanks to $121,000 in federal funds.

Bob Gibb, the bridge's namesake, was an assistant to Boise State President John Barnes. Gibb was also

DID YOU KNOW? *In addition to his work with the university, Gibb had a deep commitment to the city through his involvement with Rotary, March of Dimes, Chamber of Commerce, 4-H, Easter Seals, Masons, Neighborhood Youth Corps and other organizations. A Rotary fund named for Gibb still supports a number of local programs.*

assistant director of the university's extended day program and summer sessions. He had long advocated for the bridge.

He retired from BSU just as the bridge was nearing completion. He died on July 1, 1977, the first day of his retirement from the university,

at the age of 65. Barnes proposed naming the bridge in Gibb's honor. The City Council agreed.

Barnes and Boise Mayor Dick Eardley dedicated the bridge in October of that year. Gibb's widow, Marjorie, cut a ribbon officially opening the span.

Zoo Boise

Visitors know the zoo as a rangy place that's home to more than 250 animals from 101 species.

Because of Zoo Boise, a person can walk among iridescent blue morphos during the annual "Butterflies in Bloom" exhibition; speed past the zoo on a bike, catching a glimpse of a heavy-lidded giraffe looking back; and hear mysterious, jungly screeches echoing across the park that are utterly out of place in the Intermountain West.

A recent program even let visitors throw down their sleeping bags and spend the night among the beasts.

The zoo's origins were more modest. It opened in 1916. Its first residents: a circus refugee and a collection of rare birds given by a local sportsman's club.

As the story goes, a circus was traveling through town.

"A chimpanzee escaped. The circus left. The chimp stayed," said Liz Littman, Zoo Boise spokeswoman.

The first zookeepers were officers from the Boise Police Department. They fed the animals with food donations from local restaurants and grocery stores.

By World War II, the zoo had 40 different species. But over the next few decades, it fell into disrepair and nearly closed in 1961.

That year, the group now known as Friends of Zoo Boise formed. It has raised money and community support for the zoo and its creatures ever since.

Zoo Boise is constantly enhancing its environment with projects: a new monkey habitat (a hopeful gesture in response to a dark incident in 2012

PHOTO BY DARIN OSWALD

DID YOU KNOW? *Zoo Boise did not charge admission until 1971. The entrance fee was 35 cents for adults, 25 cents for high schoolers and 15 cents for kids. Pictured here: Ms. Mac, a zoo resident.*

when an intruder killed a resident zoo monkey) and the installation of public art works. They include a series of mosaic animals by Reham Pearson Aarti and a totem by Stephanie Inman meant to promote conservation of the hyena and the vulture — current and future zoo residents, respectively.

Magpies

"I love magpies," said Cort Conley, admitting that the birds have a bad reputation from their habit of stealing songbird eggs. Some studies have disputed this claim, according to the National Wildlife Federation. Magpie fans say the birds eat insects and rodents and dispose of carrion.

Conley, a writer and director of literature at the Idaho Commission on the Arts, said the black-billed magpie, a ubiquitous sight in local yards and parks, deserves a spot on any list of Boise icons.

"Old-timers have told me there were once bounties paid for magpies. People would collect magpie eggs, string them together and cash them in," he said.

They'd do the same with magpie legs, as recently, according to some accounts, as the mid-1970s. Today,

PHOTO BY PETE ZIMOWSKY

DID YOU KNOW? *The journals of Lewis and Clark make note of magpies that were unafraid of humans, snatching meat from the explorers' camp. Lewis and Clark admired the birds enough to send four magpies, one prairie dog and one prairie grouse back to President Thomas Jefferson at Monticello. The prairie dog and one magpie survived the trip.*

federal law protects the birds.

Conley respects the birds' savvy. They're members of the crow family. Smart. He's heard of magpies, sometimes called Mormon or Holstein pheasants, that have learned to ring doorbells for food. In a blizzard, they'll roost on the back of a

cow to stay warm. "Every magpie has different markings. They can recognize their siblings. They respect each others' borders," said Conley.

The birds lay blue green eggs. Impressionist Claude Monet's painting, "The Magpie," hangs in the Musée D'Orsay in Paris.

Christ Chapel

The interior of Christ Chapel.

Statesman reader Michael Conroy nominated Christ Chapel as a Boise icon. "When I came to Boise State in 1971, the church was very much part of the community and the site of many a Bronco marriage," said Conroy.

The church dates back to Boise's earliest days. It was one of the first Episcopal churches in the territory that's now Idaho, Utah and Montana. It's the predecessor of St. Michael's Cathedral in Downtown Boise and also has ties to the founding of Boise State University.

The Rev. Saint Michael Fackler arrived in Boise from Virginia in 1864. His congregants — miners and pioneers — wanted him to stay. He agreed on the condition that they help him build a church.

Fackler raised $2,000 in gold to build the white clapboard Gothic Revival church in 1866 at the corner of 7th and Bannock streets. After Fackler traveled back East and died during a cholera outbreak, the Boise congregation named the church St. Michael's to honor him.

In 1867, the church took on an additional role as a schoolhouse. It kept that role until St. Margaret's school for girls opened in 1892 in a building built by the Episcopal church on Idaho near 1st Street. In 1902, the St. Michael's congregation moved into its cathedral on 8th Street. Crews moved the little white church, renamed Christ Chapel, to 15th and Ridenbaugh.

St. Margaret's, in the meantime, continued to grow. In 1932, the school became co-ed. Under the guidance of Episcopal Bishop Middleton Barnwell, it changed its name to Boise Junior College and expanded into what would become Boise State University.

By the early 1960s, the fate of the little church was uncertain.

The Boise Junior College board decided it wanted the building. The Idaho Statesman paid $20,000 to restore it and move it to its current home next to Bronco Stadium.

Longtime Boise construction company Jordan-Wilcomb handled the moving. Pat Wilcomb, whose husband, Dick, worked on the project, said he found an interesting relic in the bell tower during the move: an empty whiskey bottle.

Christ Chapel today is non-denominational. Weddings, christenings and memorial services take place there. Caretakers place the church's original lace, candleholders and cross on the altar before each event. In 2012, 50 couples were married in Christ Chapel.

DID YOU KNOW? *The church's distinctive diamond-paned windows replaced the original windows in 1876.*

PHOTO BY DARIN OSWALD

Blue Turf

Boise State's blue turf is such an icon that it not only earned a spot on the Idaho Statesman's list, but was also part of the Idaho State Historical Museum's 2013 exhibition, "Essential Idaho: 150 things that make the Gem State unique," celebrating the 150th anniversary of the creation of the Idaho Territory.

When Bronco Stadium needed new AstroTurf in 1986, then-Athletic Director Gene Bleymaier had the idea to go blue. Other schools had used special colors in their end zones, but the Broncos were the first team in the world to color an entire field blue.

The trademarked turf quickly became legend. Other schools across the U.S. have followed the Bronco lead and installed colored fields. In 2012, Hosei University in Japan, which has had an academic and

PHOTO BY DARIN OSWALD

DID YOU KNOW? *Contrary to popular legend, ducks don't crash into the Bronco Stadium field, mistaking the turf for water. But at the 2009 game against the Oregon Ducks, Bronco fans wore T-shirts proclaiming, "The myth is true ... Ducks really do crash on the Blue." Boise State beat Oregon 19-8. (Pictured here: local historian and Bronco fan Amber Beierle during the Oregon game).*

cultural partnership with Boise State since 2006, got its own blue turf.

During the first 25 years of the blue turf, the Broncos won 143 of 175 matchups, further enhancing the legend of the Smurf Turf.

Buster Bronco

DID YOU KNOW? *Buster, crowd surfing in 2010, wears a No. 0 jersey for football games and a No. 54 orange jersey for basketball games.*

PHOTO PROVIDED BY BOISE STATE UNIVERSITY

Boise Junior College opened its doors in the fall of 1932 amid the Great Depression. The college's first class, 78 students taught by 15 faculty members, chose the equine mascot.

Students wanted something that paid homage to the college's western character and to the wild horses that roamed the Owyhee Canyonlands. The Bronco got the nod.

The plush Buster we know today had a predecessor.

Students began an annual tradition in 1936: building a papier mache horse, whom they named Elmer. Elmer might have been two-dimensional, but he was huge. Giant. He towered nearly as tall as a two-story building.

Students would burn him to the ground after homecoming games.

Elmer's heir, Buster Bronco, was ranked third on the Sports Illustrated Power Mascot Rankings in 2007. He was a candidate for the Capitol One Mascot of the Year for the 2008-09 season.

Velma V. Morrison Center

Harry Morrison, founder of Morrison Knudsen, and his second wife, Velma Morrison, dreamed about building a performing arts center for decades. After Harry Morrison died in 1971, Velma began rallying support for the effort.

In the 1980s, the Idaho Legislature designated $5.25 million for the center. The Harry W. Morrison Foundation gave $6.5 million. The community, including Jack and Esther Simplot, gave another $3.7 million.

Builders broke ground in 1981, and the center opened for performances in 1984.

A few notable facts about the 2,000-seat center on Boise State's campus: Original plans called for the center to be built in Ann Morrison Park near the fountain. It would have been a pyramid/ziggurat shape surrounded by parking lots. The lobby is designed for patrons to see and be seen, with lots of balconies and turns in the grand staircase. The main concert hall is designed to be tuned for individual performances like a huge musical instrument.

PHOTO PROVIDED BY BOISE STATE UNIVERSITY

DID YOU KNOW? *The Morrison Center's flyspace is 10 stories tall. Its architect, Ernest Lombard, said he didn't notice at first that the building was shaped like the state of Idaho.*

!

It has happened to more than a few of us. We have guests from out of town. We take them on a stroll through the city. They catch a glimpse of Boise Public Library with its bold and exclamatory punctuation. The cameras come out.

Some love the exclamation mark. Some wish the town would have a little more gravitas when it comes to things like library signs. Others think the exuberant mark is a perfect fit for a place where adults float down the river through the heart of town in the middle of the day on inner tubes.

By one account, the library's exclamation point reduced humorist David Sedaris to peals of laughter during a Boise visit.

The library's high-spirited punctuation has ties to pizza. When longtime Flying Pie Pizzaria owner

PHOTO BY DARIN OSWALD

DID YOU KNOW? *When signmakers installed the 5-foot exclamation marks on the main branch's two library signs in 1995, they wrapped them like giant presents. Everyone ate cakes decorated with exclamation marks.*

Howard Olivier moved to Boise in 1984, he fell in love with the Boise Public Library on Capitol Boulevard. Driving by one day, he spotted the newly installed illuminated "Library" sign on the building. He got the idea of taking the sign a step further.

After getting the library's approval, he donated the distinctive punctuation. The library began using the image throughout its branches. Sign up for a library card in Boise today, and your card will proclaim "Library!"

Oregon Trail Memorial Bridge

The span pays homage to Oregon Trail pioneers who crossed the Boise River at this spot on their way west.

In the 1920s, city leaders envisioned the bridge as a key part of the grand axis that connects the Capitol Building and the Boise Depot.

Getting the bridge built took some time. Voters failed to pass a construction bond in 1927. Federal relief dollars paid for its completion in 1931.

One hundred men worked 16-hour days for 200 straight days to build the Art Deco bridge before high-water season, according to the Idaho Heritage Trust.

The design included bronze plaques and ceramic tiles made by Works Progress Administration artists. The tiles, fired in warm, muted tones typical of the era, picture pioneer wagons and Western landscapes.

At its completion, the Idaho Statesman described the new bridge in glowing terms as a "masterful work of art" with "glistening white concrete sides that reflect the sun's rays."

The city and Ada County Highway District wanted to restore that glow for many years, said Terri Schorzman, director at the Boise Arts and History Department. The city, ACHD, Public Works and the Idaho Heritage Trust became partners in a sesquicentennial renovation.

The makeover included paint and light fixtures, tile and bronze repairs and restoration of the bridge's original light poles. The bridge once included lights that shone on the water below. Sesquicentennial plans include turning them on again after a 50-year hiatus.

DID YOU KNOW? *The design of the Oregon Trail Memorial Bridge is similar to that of the Fairview Bridge, which opened in 1932. Charles Kyle designed both bridges.*

PHOTO ABOVE BY ANNA WEBB,
PHOTO AT RIGHT BY DARIN OSWALD

Idaho Anne Frank Human Rights Memorial

PHOTO PROVIDED BY THE CITY OF BOISE

Matt Perkins, who works in the city of Boise's tree nursery, holds the sapling from Amsterdam in March 2013. City foresters will care for it and monitor its growth until it is large and strong enough to plant at the memorial site.

A special delivery arrived in Boise during its sesquicentennial year: a sapling from a horse chestnut tree that stood in the courtyard of the Amsterdam house where the Frank family hid during the Nazi occupation.

Anne's diary includes mentions of the tree. Just three months before Nazis captured her family, she wrote, "Our chestnut tree is in full bloom. It is covered with leaves and is even more beautiful than last year."

The parent tree lived for about 150 years. It stood until 2010. Toward the end of its life, arborists preserved saplings to be replanted around the world. The Idaho Anne Frank Human Rights Memorial was one of 11 sites in the U.S. chosen through a competitive process to receive a sapling. The memorial is in good company. Other recipients included

the White House, the World Trade Center site and one of the first Arkansas schools to be integrated in the 1950s.

Boise's sapling was in quarantine on the East Coast for three years, said Dan Prinzing, executive director of the Idaho Human Rights Education Center. It will stay in the care of city foresters until its trunk has grown to about 2.5 inches in diameter, said city forester Brian Jorgenson. The process will probably take a couple of years.

The chestnut sapling is one of several projects in the works at the memorial, said Prinzing. Others include an outdoor classroom, a 12-foot bronze interpretation of the chestnut tree, and a legacy garden in honor of Boise resident and Holocaust survivor Rose Beal.

The Idaho Human Rights Education Center is borrowing an idea from the Vietnam Veterans Memorial in Washington, D.C., where visitors make rubbings from names etched into the memorial's walls. A stone etched with a chestnut leaf and words from Anne Frank's diary will help visitors create mementos to take home.

The growing memorial continues to hold a special place in Boiseans' hearts. Statesman reader Jo-Ann Kachigian nominated it as a Boise icon.

"We see violations of human rights every day, both here and abroad," Kachigian wrote. The memorial's elements "offer hope as well as the opportunity to ponder what each of us can do to end such abuses. My mother was an Armenian genocide survivor. Her harrowing history inspired me to become a social justice activist. This beautiful

IDAHO STATESMAN FILE

DID YOU KNOW? *The memorial, which opened in 2002, is included in "Etched in Stone: Enduring Words from Our Nation's Monuments," a National Geographic book that highlights profound words inscribed on 52 monuments and public sites.*

place renews me."

The memorial grew out of a 1995 Anne Frank exhibit that toured Idaho. Its popularity inspired four women whom Prinzing calls the "founding mothers" — the Rev. Nancy Taylor, Leslie Drake, Marilyn Shuler and Lisa Uhlmann — to start the campaign for a permanent memorial and education center.

The Cabin

The Civilian Conservation Corps built The Cabin beside the Boise River in 1940. It housed the Idaho State Forestry Department.

The Cabin's construction, just 50 years after Idaho joined the Union in 1890, was part of the state's anniversary celebration.

The Forestry Department invited timber companies to donate wood for the project. They did, and today The Cabin has yellow pine in its entry, white pine on its main floor and red cedar in one office. The exterior logs are Englemann spruce.

The donations also saved a lot of money.

Valued at $40,000 when it was finished, the building cost taxpayers just $1,600 because of the free wood. Admirers nicknamed it the "Chateau de Bois."

DID YOU KNOW?
The Cabin is in the National Register of Historic Places. Hans Hulbe, architect for the Boise Pay-ette Lumber Co., designed it. Finnish craftsmen from Long Valley oversaw the construction.

IDAHO STATESMAN FILE

The city bought the building from the state in 1992. A group of Idaho writers founded the nonprofit Log Cabin Literary Center in 1995. They moved into the historic cabin and signed a long-term lease with the city.

The literary organization, now known as The Cabin, has maintained the building ever since.

The group and its supporters have raised more than a half-million dollars for building improvements since 2000. The Cabin hosts literary and educational programs for readers and writers.

Local writer Bill English nominated The Cabin as a Boise icon.

"What could be more iconic than a log cabin by a river that supports the language of Hemingway, Doerr and all the rest of the dedicated writers of this great city?" asked English. "The place is a temple of timbers."

Capitol Boulevard Totem Pole

The rustic building that's home to the iconic totem dates to the 1930s.

Over the years, the building has housed the New Deal Civilian Conservation Corps, a furniture showroom, a seafood restaurant called Dixon's, a tire store and a bakery. But it's the distinctive totem pole outside that's been turning heads since the 1960s.

Its carvings appear to be a wolf, a beaver, an eagle and what might be a masked man holding a fish. The carved name "Gordon" is barely visible in the chipped yellow paint at its base.

Statesman columnist Tim Woodward answered the question of the pole's origins in 2010.

A Boise native named Ed Magden opened Totem insurance agency in the building in the '60s. Magden loved Alaska. He got the pole from the Tlingit tribe and had it sent down to Boise, all the way from Ketchikan.

DID YOU KNOW? *According to one story, Boise resident Ed Magden's other additions to the building included a 10-foot Alaskan polar bear. It's unclear whether the beast was carved or stuffed.*

PHOTO BY ANNA WEBB

Ann Morrison Park

Ann Morrison, first wife of Morrison Knudsen Co. founder Harry Morrison, died in 1957. Morrison decided to build a park in her honor.

The Boise School District had optioned land between Capitol and Americana boulevards to build a new high school. But when the school bond election failed, Morrison quietly bought the 100-acre parcel — and more — to create the 153-acre park.

Morrison wanted the park built quickly. He turned the project over to veteran MK project managers. They brought heavy equipment to Boise from MK's Brownlee Dam project.

MK trucked in 15,000 yards of topsoil from the Mountain Home desert. The community donated to the project, including trees, flagpoles and other amenities. The park opened in 1959, a mere 10 months after its construction began.

One snag: Harry Morrison didn't like the original bronze image of Ann on a memorial plaque designed for the park. He hired New York City sculptor Anthony De Francisci to make a new one in 1962. De Francisci had designed the Peace Dollar for the U.S. Mint. Morrison was apparently pleased with the way De Francisci portrayed Ann. He installed the replacement portrait in the park on Feb. 23, 1963, his 78th birthday.

DID YOU KNOW? *Ann Morrison's family donated the modern clock tower that's so evocative of mid-20th century design.*

PHOTO BY JOE JASZEWSKI

Canada Geese

The large birds are undeniably distinctive. They're elegant when they saunter across a street en masse in their gray morning coats or when they perch, as they're wont to do, on the parapets of Downtown buildings, heckling passers-by.

The birds can see more than 180 degrees vertically and horizontally. Some have lived more than 20 years in the wild. They fly long and fast at a rate that would take them around the world in 40 days.

But some people wish the geese would just go away and stop pooping on everything.

Canada geese, protected by the Migratory Bird Treaty Act and other laws, have become part of the local landscape, especially in the winter, when migratory flocks mingle with resident birds and populations swell.

PHOTO BY PETE ZIMOWSKY

DID YOU KNOW? *In the wild, some geese perch on cliffs and canyon walls, hence their fondness for height.*

The city's Parks and Recreation Department has worked to manage the geese since the 1990s, enlisting all kinds of measures, including shaking and oiling eggs to prevent them from hatching, broadcasting loud noises and installing scarecrows — those coyote-like metal silhouettes that some geese appear to mock.

Other agencies use the scarecrows as well. The Idaho Transportation Department on State Street has the coyotes and a scary-looking cat with an arched back. The groundskeepers arrange the cat and coyotes into wilderness tableaux. The geese remain.

Hot Air Balloons

DID YOU KNOW? *During the city's Millenium celebration on New Year's Eve 1999, 60 hot air balloons lined Capitol Boulevard between the Boise Depot and the Capitol Building. Beginning at 11:59 p.m., one balloon lit up every second to count down the last minute of the year — and the century. Fireworks exploded over the Capitol at midnight. The display earned Boise national news coverage.*

PHOTO BY KATHERINE JONES

It's a common sensation around here. You're walking along when you sense some kind of looming presence behind you — a big, sun-blocking presence. Flocks of birds? Ghosts? Swarms of bees? No.

If you're in Boise, chances are it's a hot air balloon. Despite their size, they're eerily quiet — sometimes you can hear pilots chatting in their baskets — until their burners exhale a hot dragon breath.

The geography and stable wind patterns in the Boise Valley explain the number of balloons in Boise skies, said Scott Spencer, director of the annual Spirit of Boise Balloon Classic.

The wind comes down the canyon at Lucky Peak and over the dam into the Treasure Valley.

"But if you go up to 1,000 feet, you have a natural west to east flow that will return you to where you took off," said Spencer.

Balloon pilots call this phenomenon the "Boise Box."

The fall of 2013 will mark the 39th annual balloon rally in Boise, Spencer said.

Local ballooning began modestly in the mid-1970s. It grew steadily, reaching a high point during the years of the Boise River Festival, when balloons became synonymous with the capital city and festivity. Ballooning in Boise survived the end of the river festival.

The city's annual Spirit of Boise Balloon Classic lures pilots from around the world to fly the skies of Boise.

Why do Boiseans love their balloons so much?

"Balloons are happy," said Spencer, noting the numbers of people who show up early in the morning to see balloons launch from Ann Morrison Park.

"Balloons are not an action sport. They're pretty slow. But where else do you see people come to the park in their pajamas, drinking milk or sipping coffee to watch? It's a wholesome throwback to the '60s. It's no more complex than that — other than the fact that balloons are magic."

Boise Depot

When Shirley Maestas was growing up in Boise in the 1940s and '50s, "it was an entirely different world than it is now," she said.

Maestas lived on the Bench, but she and her friends habitually rode their bikes from one end of town to the other, from her grandmother's house at the end of Harrison Boulevard to the Foothills, which Maestas and her friends considered their big outdoor "playground." The children roamed the Capitol, too, playing hide-and-seek in the hallowed halls.

But Maestas' favorite spot in town was a perch in front of the Boise Depot from where she could survey the valley.

"We were privileged to be among the crowd that welcomed Harry Truman's campaign train on its Boise stop," Maestas said.

Truman's whistle-stop tour across the U.S. in 1948 — the close election that ended with the famous erroneous headline "Dewey Defeats Truman" — included a stop at the Boise Depot, known then as the Union Pacific Depot.

Maestas nominated the site as a Boise icon. Lisa McMillin seconded the nomination.

"I can hear the occasional train going through from my home in the North End if the weather conditions are right," she said.

Amtrak's final passenger train left the station in 1997, but Boise Valley Railroad freight trains still pass the depot twice a day — one eastbound, one westbound — carrying potatoes, lumber, fuel and fertilizer.

The California Mission-style depot opened and welcomed its first transcontinental train in 1925. City leaders had lobbied Union Pacific for years to bring the mainline to the heart of Boise. Scores of residents turned out to celebrate when that finally happened. Little girls in bonnets waved wands of apple blossoms to welcome the arriving train.

Morrison Knudsen Corp. bought the depot from Union Pacific in 1990 and began an exhaustive three-year restoration that included re-creating original light fixtures from old photographs and making the tower accessible to visitors for the first time. The company removed, cleaned and reinstalled 16,000 roof tiles — then did the same with the 45,000 brick pavers surrounding the depot.

Among the depot's original features: images of trains that decorate the waiting room ceiling trusses.

The depot became city property in 1996. It remains one of the most beloved sites in the Treasure Valley. In that way, not much has changed from when Maestas was a girl.

DID YOU KNOW?

In 1927, Union Pacific installed bells in the clock tower donated in memory of Edward Henry Harriman, former Union Pacific director. Harriman's son Averell, chairman of Union Pacific, founded the Sun Valley resort a decade later to increase ridership on Western rail lines. At right: The depot with 4th of July fireworks in 2005. The city illuminated the depot for the display.

Platt Gardens

City leaders dedicated the 7-acre Platt Gardens on the slope below the Boise Depot in the summer of 1927. That was two years after the depot opened to great fanfare.

Spanish landscape architect Ricardo Espino, who practiced in Los Angeles, designed the gardens. Original elements included winding pathways, a rock grotto, koi ponds and the panoramic view of the valley and Foothills. In the years that passenger trains came through Boise, the gardens were a popular picnic spot.

They've always been a prime destination for photographs, and continue to be, for everything from weddings to quinceaneras. Dan Everhart, Preservation Idaho spokesman, said his grandmother posed with some of her 1946 Boise High classmates for a photograph at the Platt grotto.

PHOTO BY DARIN OSWALD

DID YOU KNOW? *Platt Gardens was named for Howard V. Platt, general manager of the Oregon Short Line. Platt first proposed that Union Pacific partner with the city to build a park north of the depot.*

The gardens have an interesting past. Boise leaders bought land on the Boise Bench to be used as a railroad right of way. After Union Pacific built its spur to Boise, the city sold the leftover land, but held on to the land that became Platt Gardens.

As the era of train travel waned, the gardens fell into disrepair. The city renovated them in 2000 as a Legacy project, "restoring the now overgrown and deteriorating gardens to their original beauty," according to a 2000 press release.

Engine 2295, aka Big Mike

PHOTO BY ANNA WEBB

The American Locomotive Co. built the steam engine known as Big Mike in 1920. Big Mike traveled the Union Pacific's Main Line for decades, carrying freight from North Platte, Neb., through Fruitland and on to Huntington, Ore.

The engine hauled passenger trains between Cheyenne, Wyo., and Ogden, Utah, briefly in the 1920s, but was in freight service for most of its working life. During World War II, the locomotive carried supplies for the war effort.

Big Mike was the last steam engine to operate regularly in Southern Idaho. Union Pacific retired the engine and donated it to the city in 1959. Ownership passed to the Idaho State Historical Society in 1978.

DID YOU KNOW? *Big Mike is a 2-8-2 locomotive. That refers to the arrangement of its wheels — two on one axle, eight drive wheels on four axles, followed by two trailing wheels. Boise's Big Mike is one of only four remaining Union Pacific 2-8-2s in existence.*

The name Mike is short for Mikado, a term for a Japanese emperor. Locomotives of this type got that name because American companies first made them for export to Japan in the 1890s. The Gilbert and Sullivan opera "The Mikado" was also popular at the time and helped the nickname stick. After the attack on Pearl Harbor, the nickname MacArthur replaced Mikado on many rail lines.

After its retirement, Boise's Big Mike spent 48 years in Julia Davis Park. In 2007, the locomotive got a new home at the Boise Depot.

Artsmith's Jewelry Ring

Along with the big white horse that prances over the Pioneer Building at Main and 6th and the washer woman who toils over Cucina di Paolo, the giant diamond ring atop Artsmith's Jewelry on Vista is one of the things that makes the Boise skyline unlike any other.

Original shop owner Art Smith had the ring made when the shop opened in 1970, said current owner Rick Harvey. A third-generation Boisean, he grew up on the Bench. He started working at Artsmith's as an apprentice in 1971.

"You say Artsmith's, people say, 'Oh, that's the one with the ring on top,'" said Harvey.

A few years ago, when the ring was looking a little beat up, longtime

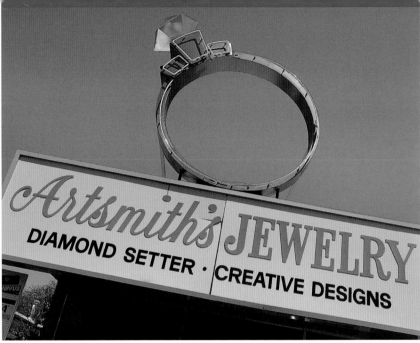

IDAHO STATESMAN FILE

DID YOU KNOW? *Vista Avenue's big ring and beloved washer woman, which once adorned the sign of a defunct laundry down the block, share a small-world story. Artsmith's owner Rick Harvey's neighbor, Andy Teague, built the washer woman in the early 1950s.*

customer Jim Cloninger rebuilt it. He charged only for materials.

The Artsmith's ring is a Tiffany-style engagement setting.

"But we haven't found anybody with a finger that fits it," said Harvey.

Lee's Candies

Lee's has always been a Nokleby family operation. L.G. Nokleby left his Idaho home as a teenager just before the turn of the 20th century. He "rode the rails" in search of adventure. He ended up learning the candy business from some of the finest candy companies in New York and San Francisco, said his grandson, Curtis Nokleby, Lee's Candies' current proprietor.

L.G. opened his first candy store in 1911 in the Dewey Palace Hotel in Nampa.

He eventually left the candy business, but convinced his son, Lee — Curtis' father — to open a candy shop on Jefferson Street (where McU Sports is today) in 1947.

Lee's moved to Vista Village on the Boise Bench in 1972.

Curtis has been a part of Lee's Candies since he was in a playpen in the back room while his parents worked. He has invented a few confections since taking over the shop — a raspberry cream, a cherry walnut cream, a sea salt caramel. But most of the candy Lee's makes uses the same recipes L.G. Nokleby brought back from his travels.

Butter almond toffee, classic caramels and most of Lee's cream centers haven't changed in decades. One of the most popular items: orange cream chocolates.

"Because I grate the whole orange into it," said Curtis.

PHOTO BY KATHERINE JONES

DID YOU KNOW? *One secret of Lee's success: "mazetta," the homemade marshmallow egg white cream that goes into Lee's cream chocolates. Curtis Nokleby doesn't worry about revealing his secrets. "Just because you have a recipe doesn't mean you can make it taste good. There's still some magic," he said.*

Betty: The Vista Washer Woman

The Maytag Laundry closed long ago. But Betty, the mechanical woman who has presided over her washtub and Vista Avenue since the 1950s, is still going strong.

Gregory Kaslo and Kay Hardy bought the former Maytag building that now houses the Cucina di Paolo in 2006. Betty came along with the deal.

"Betty is an anchor for the street," said Kaslo.

Some of Cucina di Paolo's customers share that sentiment, said restaurant owner Paul Wegner. For some, she's assumed idol status. She's a spiritual presence.

"A lady came in and said if the washer woman was gone, all of Boise would vanish," said Wegner.

Statesman reader David Klinger had another take on Betty: "Every time I fly back into Boise and make the drive down Vista, the faithful washer woman reminds me that when I return home, there'll be dirty laundry for me to do."

Bench resident Andy Teague built Betty in the 1950s. Kaslo and Hardy hired retired pilot and metal fabricator Bruce Whittig to rebuild the plywood, foam and chicken-wire Betty. He made her operational again after a 15-year hiatus, fitting her with "space-age" joints.

"She'll last longer than we will," Whittig said.

He still cares for Betty, who's about 5 feet tall when she's standing straight. Betty's dresses change with the seasons, courtesy of the Boise State University theater department. Fitting them requires laying yards of fabric out like a Mercator projection,

PHOTO BY DARIN OSWALD

DID YOU KNOW? *Besides Betty, the washer woman has been known as Maude, Bridget, Doris, Sadie and Wanda.*

climbing ladders and fastening them to Betty with Velcro.

"To the sound of hoots and car horns," Whittig said.

Betty has been on the job for more than 60 years. Retirement is not in her future.

"But when it gets hotter than 100 degrees outside, a circuit turns her off. We call it union rules," said Kaslo.

'Sally Reed Lived Here' Marker

A modest stone monument in front of the Idaho Angler shop on Vista Avenue marks the spot where Sally Reed's home once stood. Her Supreme Court victory in 1971 blazed a trail for American women's rights.

Reed v. Reed marked the first time that the court applied the Equal Protection Clause of the 14th Amendment to strike down a state law that discriminated against women.

After Sally Reed and her husband, Cecil, divorced in 1958, she supported herself and her teenage son, Skip, who was found dead in his father's basement in 1967. The death was ruled a suicide.

Both Reed and her ex-husband filed petitions to administer Skip's estate, which included a record collection and a college savings account of $495.

Idaho law stated at the time that "the male must be preferred over the female" in cases where both parties are equally qualified. The local judge automatically approved Cecil Reed's application, and Sally Reed decided to appeal.

After 16 lawyers turned her down, Boise lawyer Allen Derr agreed to represent her. The case went all the way to the Supreme Court. Future Justice Ruth Bader Ginsburg wrote the brief.

On Nov. 22, 1971, Chief Justice Warren Burger wrote the opinion for the court, which was unanimous in Sally Reed's favor. The ruling helped overturn similar laws across the U.S.

Sally Reed lived in the house on Vista Avenue until it was torn down in 1999. She died in Boise in 2002 at age 93. She is buried at Cloverdale Memorial Park next to her son.

Allen Derr, who died in 2013, paid for the monument.

DID YOU KNOW?

You can read more about Sally Reed's case in the book "Days of Destiny: America's Greatest Historians Examine Thirty-one Days that Changed the Course of History."

PHOTO BY ANNA WEBB

Morris Hill Cemetery

Morris Hill Cemetery, with its massive trees, shady expanses and the mist that appears on very cold mornings and very hot afternoons, is a place of considerable beauty.

Like lots of Boise neighborhoods, it's an equal-opportunity kind of place, a mix of the grand and the modest.

The imposing markers of Sens. William Borah (died 1940) and Frank Church (1984) aren't far from the simple marker on the grave of gubernatorial assassin Harry Orchard that reads "The Man God Made Again." Orchard died in 1954.

Magnates Joe Albertson (1993) and J.R. Simplot (2008) are buried at Morris Hill. So is "Peg Leg" Annie Morrow, owner of gold rush "houses of entertainment" in Atlanta and Rocky Bar. She lost her feet to

frostbite but lived to be 75. She was buried at Morris Hill in 1934.

The stone of James Jesus Angleton, the Boise-born director of counterintelligence for the CIA during the 1970s, stands a short walk from the field set aside for the indigent men and women that Ada County pays to bury.

The cemetery contains various sections, including those for St. John's Cathedral, for Ahavath Beth Israel and for fraternal organizations. There's an Islamic section and an Asian section.

Morris Hill has three sections devoted to the military. Several anonymous graves of soldiers lie throughout the military sections.

One irony: The city placed the Asian section in what was initially an out-of-the-way corner of the cemetery.

The construction of Americana Boulevard after World War II made the Asian section at Latah and Emerald one of the cemetery's most prominent.

For a time between 1906 and the late 1920s, the Boise Valley Railroad Co. ran a special funeral street car hearse to carry coffins to the cemetery.

William Lindsay, 15, was the first person buried at Morris Hill after the cemetery opened in 1882. According to cemetery records, he died what must have been a difficult death from "scrofula," a tuberculous infection of the lymph nodes in his neck.

You can find his grave amid other Lindsay stones in the cemetery's oldest section near the corner of Roosevelt and Emerald. The stone, adorned by a pair of clasped hands, isn't vertical anymore. It's not located exactly where records say it is, but it's worth the search.

Some other causes of death listed in the burial record the year young Lindsay died: snow slide, gunshot, poison, falling tree, falling rock, steel car accident and la grippe — another term for influenza.

Boise Mayor James Pinney was responsible for the cemetery. In the 1880s, Pioneer Cemetery on Warm Springs was the city's main burial ground. Pinney wanted a larger cemetery. He paid $2,000 of the city's money to buy 80 acres on the Boise Bench from landowners William Ridenbaugh and Lavinia I. Morris, widow of William Morris, for whom the area was named.

At the time, the purchase was controversial. More than a century later, Boiseans regard the cemetery as hallowed historic ground and one of the city's most accessible records of its residents.

PHOTO BY DARIN OSWALD

DID YOU KNOW? *In the 1990s, members of the Basque community spent years matching death records to unmarked Basque burial sites in the cemetery. In 1997, Dorothy Aldecoa, who grew up in a Basque boarding house in Emmett, paid for 60 individual markers as well as a large stone monument in the cemetery's St. John's section that lists the names of Basques whose graves could not be positively identified.*

Ahavath Beth Israel Synagogue

Jews have had a presence in Boise since the city's earliest days. An Idaho Statesman story from 1869 detailed Yom Kippur services held at the Masonic Lodge Downtown.

Ahavath Beth Israel is the oldest synagogue in continuous use west of the Rockies.

Pioneers built the Moorish-style synagogue in 1895. Its founders included Moses Alexander, who became the mayor of Boise and the governor of Idaho — one of the first Jewish governors in the U.S.

In the early 1900s, the synagogue, then known as Beth Israel, served as a haven for disenfranchised groups. Congregation member Sherrill Livingston said that when the first Latter-day Saints arrived in Boise, only the Jewish community opened its doors to them.

PHOTO BY JOE JASZEWSKI

Harriet Badescheim, right, embraces Gretchen Hecht after the synagogue's move from Downtown Boise in 2003.

Today's Congregation Ahavath Beth Israel is the result of two synagogues merging. After World War II, Jews in the military arrived at Gowen Field and Mountain Home Air Force Base. They built Ahavath Israel, a more conservative synagogue, at 27th and Bannock.

The congregations came together in 1986.

Ahavath Beth Israel moved from its original site at 11th and State streets to the Boise Bench in a dramatic, middle-of-the-night trip in 2003. Moving the 60-ton building took six hours. During the move, crews discovered documentation showing that Marshall Field and Levi Strauss & Co. contributed to the synagogue's original construction.

The congregation restored its rose window and several smaller windows in 2012. Workers painstakingly disassembled the windows into approximately 1,000 pieces.

The windows traveled to Portland, where glass restorer David Schlicker repaired them. This was a challenge, since some of the colors in the 117-year-old windows are no longer produced commercially.

Schlicker had to find replacements in his extensive glass collection, amassed over 35 years in the business.

The Bench

A homestead built in 1887 near what's now Curtis Road was one of the Bench's first residences, according to city historians. Morris Hill Cemetery, now a Bench institution, had been open just five years at that point.

Canals and irrigation brought more homesteaders to the Boise Bench after the turn of the century, along with the railway and the splendid Union Pacific depot built in 1925. Developments along what's now Crescent Rim and Hulbe Drive began to grow in the 1930s. Homes here were among the first in Boise to take advantage of the valley's dramatic vistas.

But the area's character really began to shift in the 1940s. The establishment of Gowen Field as a military airfield meant thousands of

PHOTO BY ANNA WEBB

DID YOU KNOW? *By the 1950s, 30,000 Boiseans, or half the city's population, lived south of the Boise River in "post-war suburbia." The military decommissioned Sergeant City in 1946. In 2011, the Boise Architecture Project included Sergeant City on its list of the most endangered historic sites in the city.*

new residents for Boise. In 1941, the Federal Works Agency built Sergeant City, a 100-unit complex for military families north of Overland Road and off Latah Avenue.

The development — whose main

streets, Pershing and Cushing, hint at its military origins — included a mix of small houses, apartments and playgrounds. It is partially intact today, though it is no longer a military complex.

Sergeant City was one of Boise's first "modern" residential suburbs. It was also a harbinger of the kinds of developments that would proliferate on the Bench.

In the boom years after the war, Boiseans, like Americans everywhere, fell in love with their cars and the mobility those cars offered. Car ownership meant people could live far from where they worked. Suburban life, with its airy homes, carports and big yards, was born. The Bench, with its open expanses of land near — but not too near — the city, was the perfect place for this new sensibility.

It's appropriate, considering the growing car culture, that Boise's first McDonald's drive-thru opened on the Bench on Orchard Street in 1961.

The Day family, which arrived in Boise in 1915 and opened a real estate development company, capitalized on the city's growing interest in suburban life. The firm developed Vista Village in 1949. It was Idaho's first planned residential and shopping district outside the city's core. The street-side parking lot offered plenty of spaces for drivers.

The firm also developed a number of suburban enclaves on the Bench in the 1950s, including Mesa Vista, Hillcrest Terrace and others. Today, architectural historians love the Bench for its many examples of mid-century design. The city annexed the area in the early 1960s.

Long before people arrived, the Bench was all about geology.

Because Boise is such a big bike town, people tend to be aware of geology in a way they might not have to be in other cities, said Sam Matson, lecturer in the Department of Geosciences at Boise State University.

"Every time you ride up onto the Bench, up Prospect or Americana, or Broadway onto Federal Way, you definitely know that you're on a hill," Matson said.

Geologically speaking, the Bench is a river terrace, a "stair step" formation left by the Boise River as it cut through the Treasure Valley a few hundred thousand years ago, he said.

The Downtown core and Boise State campus are technically on a bench as well — just a lower, newer bench cut during the last ice age, between 13,000 and 25,000 years ago.

All of this happened long after Lake Idaho, the shallow body of water that filled the valley 5 million years ago, had drained away through Hells Canyon.

Hap Tallman Stockman's Supply

Hap Tallman's celebrated its 50th anniversary in 2012 with a barbecue and a mechanical bull in its parking lot on Overland.

When Hap Tallman opened his store in 1962, the road outside was oil and gravel, said his daughter-in-law, Carol Tallman. Hap Tallman, who is no longer living, went into business to cater to cattle ranchers and others with farm operations nearby. At first, he sold only animal vaccines and feed.

"But he started hiring rodeo kids in the late '60s," said Carol. "And they talked him into carrying colored rodeo hats."

PHOTO BY JOE JASZEWSKI

That led to a full line of Western clothes, boots and horse tack — some of it festooned with fringe and rhinestones. The store and other businesses of its era, such as Flynn's Saddle Shop on State Street that opened in 1958, are iconic remnants of a Western lifestyle that's ever-rarer in the capital city.

The store still keeps small amounts of animal feed on hand for die-hard customers who don't want to buy it elsewhere. Hats of every style line the walls of Hap Tallman's. Low crowns and wide "shovel" brims are in style these days, said Carol.

She's worked at the store for 41 years and has seen styles change. When it comes to boots, cowboys are now favoring those with wide, square toes. The shelves of boots include alligator and ostrich boots with $400 price tags. But they also include boots with glow-in-the-dark skulls and costume footwear for participants in cowboy action shooting. The pastime requires period garb and is more and more popular, said Carol.

On any given day, a visitor to the store might find Jed Rice, 20, making a pair of custom chaps in the store's workshop. Rice works intently on a counter in front of rolls of colored, fragrant leather. A jar nearby holds the tools he uses to stamp intricate patterns into leather.

"He's a master," said Carol.

The shop's website includes this motto (Carol Tallman isn't sure of its origins):

"We have made money. We have

PHOTO BY ANNA WEBB

DID YOU KNOW? *Jed Rice made his first pair of chaps when he was just 14. The store has made chaps (pronounced with a soft "ch" like chaparral) for rodeo riders and rodeo queens for decades. Chaps availability, according to the website, is subject to "demand and customer attitude."*

cashed bad checks, etc. We have been cussed and discussed, knocked, talked about, lied about and lied to, held up and robbed. The only reason we stay in business is to see what the hell will happen next!"

USS Boise

The story of the USS Boise, a World War II light cruiser, "pops up with all these famous characters and famous battles," said Ken Swanson, director of the Idaho Military History Museum.

The USS Boise was commissioned in 1938. When Japan bombed Pearl Harbor in 1941, the ship was already in the Philippines.

"So it was in the war from Day One," said Swanson.

Just months after Pearl Harbor, the U.S. wanted to send a message to Japan. The Doolittle raid in April 1942 was the first U.S. air strike on the island nation. The USS Boise, positioned near Japan's southern islands, sent out radio chatter to distract Japanese military away from the mainland.

Months later, the ship faced its most deadly encounter, Cape Esperance on Guadalcanal. Within the first minutes of battle, a Japanese heavy cruiser hit the USS Boise, killing more than 140 men, said Swanson. It made it back to the Philadelphia Navy yards for repair.

The USS Boise had some intriguing encounters. It impressed Gen. George Patton with its firepower at the Battle of Gela in 1943 during the Allied invasion of Sicily. When Gen. Douglas MacArthur returned to liberate the Philippines in 1944, Swanson said, he rode on the USS Boise.

In 1945, when the war in Europe had ended, the USS Boise was part of a happier mission: The U.S. sent every available ship to Europe to pick up military personnel and bring them home.

The Navy took the ship out of action in 1946. It sat "in mothballs" for a few years until Argentina bought it for its Navy. After the Falklands War, Argentina sold the ship for scrap. It was towed to Texas and cut up.

"It's now in razor blades and cars all over the world," said Swanson.

The USS Boise may be gone from all but memory and photographs, but remnants exist. Until about 10 years ago, veterans who served on the ship held regular reunions in Boise. The ship's original bell, repaired after the battle on Guadalcanal, is at the Idaho Military History Museum.

A monument stands next to the Discovery Center of Idaho on Myrtle Street. Given by the citizens of Boise, it lists the names of the "officers and men of the United States Ship Boise who engaged in gallant action off Cape Esperance ..."

DID YOU KNOW? *The USS Boise, pictured here, has a descendant. A Navy submarine launched in 1991 inherited the USS Boise name. The ship took part in Operation Enduring Freedom and Operation Iraqi Freedom. Boise Mayor David Bieter attended a change-of-command ceremony in 2013 for the USS Boise in Virginia. The Navy often decorates the submarine in blue and orange, a nod to the Boise State Broncos.*

Boise LDS Temple

The Church of Jesus Christ of Latter-day Saints' Boise Temple was the second LDS temple built in Idaho, after the Idaho Falls Temple, constructed in 1945. Gordon B. Hinckley, who later became church president, dedicated Boise's six-spired, marble-clad structure in 1984.

In the summer of 2011, the Boise Temple closed for a 15-month remodel of its interior and grounds. Its four-week public open house in the fall of 2012 drew 170,000 visitors from 41 states and 12 countries, said Brian Whitlock, area director for the church.

The temple is reserved for the church's highest sacraments, including marriages. Once a temple is dedicated, it's open only to members of the faith who live according to certain church standards.

The design of a temple reflects local culture and its physical surroundings, said Whitlock. The shape of the Art Deco temple in Idaho Falls reflects the rocky, jagged walls of the Snake River canyons, for example.

Because Boise is the City of Trees, tree motifs are present throughout its temple. The baptistry features a wall of stained glass with a botanical theme. The wall, in jewel tones of green and blue, is made of 4,500 individual pieces of glass. The leaves on the trees are hand-cut crystal with beveled edges.

Visitors will find water imagery as well, reminiscent of the Boise River or the living water of Jesus Christ, said Whitlock. Stylized blossoms of the syringa, Idaho's state flower, are also prominent — another nod to the local landscape. Some of the

blossoms contain glass fragments recycled from the temple's original stained glass.

The 2011 remodel included replacing the 8-foot-tall statue of Moroni, prophet of the Book of Mormon, atop the temple's tallest spire. The statue is leafed in 24-karat gold. A polyurethane coating should protect it from the elements for at least another 28 years, said Whitlock.

All aspects of temple construction must reach a level of perfection, said Chris Bergevin, one of the craftsmen who helped install stone and tile.

During one part of the project, his crew spent three days laying tile in the hallway between the men's and women's dressing rooms. Officials came in after the job was almost done and told the tile setters that the tile had to be set at a 90-degree

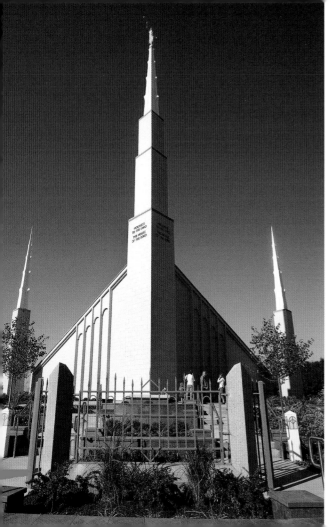

angle, not square. "So we took it all out and did it again," said Bergevin.

They broke only a couple of tiles in the process. The new floor is sometimes covered with a rug. That doesn't matter.

"We went to the trouble to make sure it was perfect anyway," said Bergevin.

The church is designing a fifth Idaho temple that will be built in Meridian. The third temple was built in Rexburg. The fourth in Twin Falls. Meridian's temple is scheduled to be finished between 2015 and 2017.

"We're more interested in doing it right than in doing it fast," Whitlock said.

The 2011 Boise renovation opened up the temple grounds to make them more welcoming.

"That's intentional," said Whitlock. "We'd love for anyone to come and enjoy the peace and serenity of being there."

Intermountain Gas

The Idaho Statesman ran an article in 1950 about the El Paso Natural Gas Co.'s plans to build a pipeline through Idaho. A Boise couple, Nat and Myrtis Campbell, read the piece. They saw the new pipeline as an opportunity to start a local natural gas distribution company.

Nat Campbell pulled a group of investors, bankers and businesspeople together. They named themselves Intermountain Gas.

"The Campbells were not the only ones with the idea," said Byron Defenbach, a company spokesman.

Their group had to compete with others who wanted the franchise to tap into the pipeline. The Idaho Legislature had the task of decid-

STATESMAN ARCHIVE PHOTO FROM THE BOISE STATE UNIVERSITY SPECIAL COLLECTIONS

DID YOU KNOW? *The "roundhouse" pictured is the company's mechanical room, housing its heating and cooling operations. Originally, the roundhouse included a natural gas-fired turbine to generate electricity. It powered the complex, allowing it to be independent of other local power sources. Repair costs in the 1970s were prohibitive, so the complex hooked up to the electric grid.*

ing which group should get it, and decided on the Campbells. Competitors appealed to the Idaho Supreme Court, which backed the Legislature.

Intermountain Gas opened in 1955, operating out of a plumbing contractor's office Downtown. The

company's first customer was Farmer Dell, an applesauce company in New Plymouth near the pipeline route.

The first Boise natural gas customer was a barber shop on Main Street not far from the Egyptian Theatre. A photo shows Intermountain staffers crowded into a tiny alleyway among garbage cans to see the natural gas valve turned on for the first time. By the end of 1955, Intermountain Gas had five customers, including the Green Giant plant in Buhl, the Payette Creamery and the private home of the mayor of New Plymouth.

Intermountain Gas opened a showroom on Idaho Street in Boise to demonstrate the modern wonders of natural gas, including cooking Simplot french fries.

"Everyone had been cooking with electricity, so this was a brave new world," said Defenbach.

In that spirit, the company bought farmland, roughly 10 acres, on Cole Road in 1959 for $45,000. The plan was to build a state-of-the-art headquarters.

The company hired Spokane architect Kenneth Brooks to design the complex. Longtime Boise construc-

tion company Jordan-Wilcomb began construction in 1964. The building won a national design award from the American Institute of Architects. The company is restoring the exterior bricks, which are various hues of green, gray, blue and purple.

"This was meant to be a showplace, looking to the future," said Defenbach.

Today, it looks like a stage set from "Mad Men." Much of the original complex, along with its furniture, is intact. That includes a lounge chair and ottoman designed in 1956 by Charles and Ray Eames for Herman Miller. The company bought it new in 1964 for $600 (it still has the receipt). The set, made with Brazilian rosewood and stuffed with goose down, is appraised at $5,000.

Idaho Statesman

The Statesman has told its readers about presidential assassinations and wartime victories. The paper announced statehood in 1890 with the words, "Let the Eagle Scream!"

Readers have turned to the Statesman to learn about the sinking of the Titanic, the bombing of Pearl Harbor and the opening of the completed State Capitol on a cold day in 1921. The Statesman announced Neil Armstrong's lunar stroll in 1969.

The paper's history reaches back to Boise's earliest days. A year after the city was platted, the Idaho Tri-Weekly Statesman produced its first issue from a windowless log cabin with a dirt floor where City Hall sits today. The driving force behind the first paper was H.C. Riggs. He came to the Boise Valley with his family in 1863 and helped lay out Boise's first

PHOTO PROVIDED BY IDAHO STATE HISTORICAL SOCIETY, 1239-D

Idaho Statesman journalists and pressmen from the paper's early days.

city plan. In 1864, he was elected to the Idaho Territory Legislature, then meeting in Lewiston. His powers of persuasion were so great, he helped convince delegates to move the capital to Boise and to create a county named for his daughter, Ada.

That done, Riggs turned his attention to newspapers. He offered New Yorker James Reynolds $1,500 and the Main Street cabin to settle in Boise instead of Idaho City. At the time, Idaho City had more than four times as many people as Boise. Reyn-

DID YOU KNOW? *The Statesman is still on the lookout for original copies of the April 27, 1865, Idaho Tri-Weekly Statesman announcing the assassination of President Abraham Lincoln (12 days after it happened, which gives a sense of how slowly news traveled in those days). This issue has proved elusive throughout the decades. Historians believe the assassination was such huge news that the issue disappeared into family scrapbooks.*

The front page from the first issue, July 26, 1864, and the July 7, 2013, front page marking the city's sesquicentennial.

olds, an abolitionist and supporter of Abraham Lincoln, took the offer and became the paper's first publisher.

The inaugural issue of the Statesman hit Boise streets on July 26, 1864.

Almost half of the front page was devoted to Civil War news — "Particulars of the Great Raid into Maryland" and "Rebels Repulsed at Bush Hill." Advertisements were mostly those for Idaho City lawyers.

The first paper had the beginnings of a humor column. A brief equated the sight of a polka-dancing man to a man shaking loose change down the leg of his trousers.

Reynolds was aware of the risk of starting a newspaper in a nascent city 300 miles from the nearest mail delivery. Days after the first paper was printed, he wrote an editorial:

"OUR PAPER: No one who has never had the trial can fully appreciate the labor and perseverance and untiring care required to start a newspaper and get it in successful operation. It is a rough business in any country, and the failures outnumber the successes. But in our humble opinion this country, as we found it, is about as rough a place to start this business as any poor Knight of the quill or stick ever stumbled upon."

The paper has had several homes, including a clapboard building that followed the cabin on the northwest corner of 6th and Main, the brick building that still stands on the southwest corner of 6th and Main, and the building on the northeast corner of 6th and Bannock streets, designed by Pietro Belluschi in 1951. The Statesman moved into its current building, designed by Charles Hummel, on Curtis Road in 1972.

Chapter Three WEST BOISE/NORTH END

Spaulding Ranch

The 20-acre expanse of open space and shade trees off North Cole Road is iconic for a few reasons.

The Spaulding Ranch, uninhabited for many years, is among the last remaining open farmland within Boise city limits.

Around the turn of the 20th century, farms like the Spauldings' were common. Today, the site is the exception. It became one of the city's nine historic preservation districts in 1996. It is the only district consisting of a single property and the only district with an agricultural character.

Almon and Mary Spaulding homesteaded the farm in 1896. At that time, the farm covered 100 acres, about five times its current size. Owners have sold or donated acreage through the years, including land that became the Capital High School ballfield.

The Spaulding Ranch is in the National Register of Historic Places. Its application for the designation noted the farm's outbuildings. They include a classic red barn with a double-pitched roof that dates to 1910. Other historic structures include a farmhouse, a wooden silo and a New Deal-era outdoor toilet built in the spirit of sanitizing rural America.

Harvey and Katherine Caron bought the former Spaulding farmstead in the 1940s. The Idaho Statesman featured the Carons in a 1954 society page feature titled, "Life in the country includes irrigatin' for these once-city dwellers." Katherine Caron spent many years as a fashion buyer for the C.C. Anderson department store chain.

The Spauldings' land was a working farm until the mid-1990s. A renter kept 20 head of Holstein and grew hay there. Katherine Caron campaigned to get the ranch listed in the National Register. She died in 2012 at the age of 100.

An Idaho investment firm bought the property. To build at Spaulding Ranch, a developer would have to convince the Historic Preservation Commission to remove the designation from the site, or part of the site.

The idea that this could happen one day inspired the Boise Architecture Project to list the Spaulding Ranch in 2010 as one of the most endangered historic sites in the city.

T.C. Bird Planetarium

The planetarium at Capital High School presented its first program shortly after it opened in 1969. The Star of Bethlehem program has been an annual tradition ever since.

That program explores what stars were shining in the sky some 2,000 years ago when the wise men traveled to Jerusalem.

For many school kids across the Treasure Valley, field trips to the T.C. Bird Planetarium were, and are, among the best of the year.

"The lights go off, the stars come on. You feel like you're in a different world," said Tom Campbell, director of the planetarium.

The planetarium owes its existence to advocacy from then-Superintendent of Schools T.C. Bird, for whom it's named, and the Apollo space program (1961-1975). Apollo made scientific and astronomical pursuits part of American popular culture.

Half of the money to build the planetarium came from the federal government, which was funding lots of science programs across the U.S. at that time, Campbell said.

The other half came from the district after voters approved a bond on its second try.

The planetarium is one of a few in Idaho. Capital is one of only three high schools in the Northwest with such a facility.

It's always been open to students from around the Valley, Campbell said. In its heyday, 30,000 students attended programs there each year. These days, because of budget cuts that make it hard for schools to afford the $35 fee for each presentation, plus bus fare, only about 12,000 visit annually.

But those who do make it enjoy programs tailored to their grade level.

Third-graders, the youngest visitors, get an introduction to the night sky — constellations they can walk outside and see that very night — and a lesson about the planets.

On the other end of the spectrum, high school students in AP classes get programs on physics, the theory of relativity and the relationship between chemicals on earth and their relation to star evolution.

With just 57 seats under its 30-foot dome, the planetarium is an intimate space. Architects designed it to accommodate just two classes at a time.

When adults who visited the planetarium as kids come back, Campbell hears a common refrain: "This was much bigger when I was little."

Merritt's Scones

The classic Merritt's scone is a flying saucer of warm dough with an orb of melting honey butter — more Indian fry bread than British tea confection.

Delicious, yes. There for you in your time of need, yes.

Cooks at Merritt's fry scones around the clock. The cafe is open nearly 24/7. It closes Sunday nights at 10 p.m. but is open again at 6 a.m. every Monday morning.

The Merritt family took over the former Yatesville truck stop in 1975 on what was then the outskirts of town. They started making scones as a cheaper alternative to bread, said proprietor George Merritt. For a long time, the cafe was known for its biscuits and gravy. But in the past 20 years, scones have become the big draw.

Growing up in Boise in the 1980s, going to Merritt's was standard practice at the end of a night of dancing at the Crazy Horse, driving around the hills, or standing around at Bronco Stadium during cold Friday night high school football games. Those are the youthful moments when hunger for something warm and fried becomes a kind of desperation.

Things haven't changed much at Merritt's, said server Rhonda Bothke.

"You come here at midnight and it's all kids with milkshakes and scones," she said.

Merritt's is popular with people on their way to the racetrack and with "skiers coming in for their ritual breakfasts," said Merritt.

Portraits of horses hang on the walls. Framed photos remind patrons

PHOTO BY DARIN OSWALD

DID YOU KNOW? *Original owner Les Merritt (George Merritt's dad) died in 2013 at the age of 85. "He was born the same year the Yatesville truck stop opened," said George. "We liked to say that they were both 1928 models."*

of a time when State Street was a sleepy, two-lane road and the acres behind Merritt's were pastures, not subdivisions.

Smoky Davis

This writer's snapshots of a Boise childhood: Shooting cap guns, leaving the smell of sulfur in the air while sporting a fringed leather vest that could either go "hippie" or "cowgirl"; dividing my thoughts between the existence of Bigfoot and the exploits of Evel Knievel; and looking forward to Christmas and the appearance of a bag of Smoky Davis beef jerky in my Christmas stocking.

Smoky Davis, in the hands of the Davis family for three generations, still makes the blessed jerky. The recipe hasn't changed since 1953, when Dell Davis, the original Smoky, opened his doors on State Street.

The Davises, Dell's grandson Gary and his wife, Dee, preside over a case of smoked meats and cheeses.

PHOTO PROVIDED BY SMOKY DAVIS

DID YOU KNOW? *Smoky Davis' iconic neon sign — some of the most recognizable script around for longtime Boiseans — is grandfathered. Were the business to open today, the Davises couldn't advertise with such a big sign, said Dee Davis.*

The Davises smoke the meat they sell on-site, a process that hasn't changed in six decades. They'll custom smoke "anything," said Dee.

Dell Davis was an all-around entrepreneur. He had his own plane. He ran a bar in Mountain Home for a time. He became a partner at Robinson Quick Freeze, a business that offered freezer space for rent. Customers started asking Dell to smoke the meat they brought in. Davis decided to open his own smoke shop on State Street. Bankers advised him against it.

"They didn't think it would work," said Dee.

Dell opened anyway. He started smoking meats and gathering a loyal clientele. Sixty years later, the Davises continue to prove that Dell was right and the bankers were wrong.

MK Bucyrus-Erie B3

This historic shovel, built in Milwaukee in the 1920s, is a connection to the early days of Boise-born Morrison Knudsen Co.

Harry Morrison and Morris Knudsen founded their construction and engineering company in 1912. As legend has it, the two began with $600, some horses, a few wheelbarrows and Fresno scrapers — machines that moved dirt to build canals and ditches.

But by the 1950s, MK had major projects around the world, including the Hoover and Grand Coulee dams and the San Francisco Bay Bridge. Time magazine recognized Morrison in 1954 as "the man who has done more than anyone else to change the face of the earth."

Morrison Knudsen diversified in the following decades into the space program, mining and more.

The Bucyrus-Erie B3 harks back to a more modest time. The company bought it in 1931 (around the same time MK was starting work on the Hoover Dam) for just over $9,000.

The shovel is notable for its wooden cab and tracks akin to those on a tank. Historians believe MK put it to work building canals and railroads in the local area.

The B3 stood on the former MK Plaza at Broadway Avenue and Park Boulevard through the company's reincarnations into Washington Group International and then URS Corp.

After URS offered to donate the B3, the Idaho Transportation Department gave it a new home. In 2012, movers loaded the B3 onto a lowboy trailer and carried it across town to ITD's State Street

headquarters. An official there fondly described the B3 as one of a "vanishing breed of workhorses."

Another MK-related site is the Wake Island Memorial in Veterans Memorial Park. The city and local veterans dedicated it in 2011 to honor those who fought and were taken prisoner in the Battle of Wake Island, just after the attack on Pearl Harbor. That included more than 1,000 civilian MK employees who were building a military base on the island.

The 4-foot-tall sandstone memorial exists thanks to the efforts of Noah Barnes, who worked on the memorial for his Eagle Scout award. His great-grandfather, MK employee Loren H. Hance, was captured on Wake Island and died in a Japanese prison. The U.S. government recognized the civilians as veterans in 1981.

DID YOU KNOW?

The Bucyrus-Erie B3 sits near the entrance of the Idaho Transportation Department. The building, built in 1961, is historically significant in its own right. Boise architect Charles Hummel designed it in the international style, one that became popular in the mid-20th century.

PHOTO BY
KATHERINE JONES

165

Lowell Pool

DID YOU KNOW? *The Lowell Pool is a remnant in a neighborhood that was once home to the Lowell Grocery and Hamburger Korner across from the pool on 28th Street. Hamburger Korner was home to the Bellybuster, by some local accounts the best burger ever made. In this photo, neighbors celebrate the pool's 50th anniversary in 2003.*

IDAHO STATESMAN FILE

In the summer of 1953, the city of Boise offered kids a pretty good selection of entertainment options. There were supervised playgrounds at Garfield, Whitney, Franklin, Jefferson and other elementary schools. Julia Davis Park had tennis and archery programs. North and South junior highs offered dance and art classes. Little kids could join the city's baseball program, signing up for the "Knothole," "Junior Knothole," "Midget," "Thumper Major" or "Thumper Minor" leagues. There was even something called "patriotic day."

But the big thrill that summer, when radios were blasting hits such as Hank Williams' "Your Cheatin' Heart," must have been when Lowell Pool opened on North 28th Street. The pool had a full house, 250 swimmers, on opening night. With its stucco facade that's somehow reminiscent of a Jazz Age movie theater, Lowell is one of the city's oldest public pools. South Pool on Shoshone Street opened a week later on the Boise Bench.

Both define "neighborhood pool," though they're part of the citywide Boise Parks and Recreation system.

The city has considered closing both old pools at different times through the years. They're not big money-makers.

According to an Idaho Statesman story, the city expected each pool to cost about $50,000 to operate in 2013.

Some city leaders say the pools are in areas with a high percentage of kids from low-income families who don't have a lot of other options.

For many residents, Lowell Pool — all 30 yards of it — is an irreplaceable part of the city fabric.

When Lowell Pool turned 50, the city celebrated with cake, games and a reunion of former lifeguards.

Statesman columnist and North End native Tim Woodward attended the reunion. He wrote fondly of his days as a Lowell "pool rat." He recalled an "insanely beautiful" female lifeguard named Kip and a convenient tree limb that may — or may not — have helped him and fellow pool rats get into the pool before swim season officially began at the end of the school year.

Lowell Elementary

Boise has its share of historic elementary schools: Washington was built in 1911, Longfellow in 1906 and Collister in 1912, and there are others.

Lowell, built in 1913 in Boise's North End, is an iconic example of a thriving Boise neighborhood school. When the city marked its sesquicentennial in 2013, the Leopards of Lowell celebrated their centennial.

Here are some facts about Lowell's first century: The school was named for Harvard graduate James Russell Lowell. He was a romantic poet, critic, editor and diplomat. He held anti-slavery views. His writings inspired Mark Twain.

Sand Creek ran along the edge of the playground. This meant muddy kids and, occasionally, a flooded

PHOTO BY KATHERINE JONES

DID YOU KNOW? *At the 1944 school carnival, attendees paid a dime for a chance to win a $25 War Bond.*

school basement.

In 1944, eight fathers made 10 tables at a cost of $40 for the lunchroom, which doubled as the school gym. Before this, the school borrowed lunch tables from Hotel Boise.

In 1977, gardeners planted a special pine tree on the Lowell playground. The Moon Tree grew from seeds that astronauts had taken to the moon and back. Just three moon trees were planted in Idaho.

Marian Pritchett School

The first officers of the Salvation Army arrived in Boise, population 3,500, in 1887.

In 1921, the organization opened The Salvation Army Rescue Home (later called the Booth Home), a small "lying-in," or maternity, hospital in the North End for unwed mothers.

The home was part of a larger international network. Minister William Booth founded The Salvation Army in London's East End in 1865. Soon after, the organization opened its first homes for poor women, many of whom were pregnant. The first American rescue home opened in Brooklyn in 1887. Ten rescue homes, including Boise's, opened in the West in the next few decades.

In 1963, the Idaho Legislature passed a bill authorizing pay for teachers to teach academic classes. In 1964,

DID YOU KNOW? *A large mural on campus made by students features stars, birds, butterflies and an image of a child riding a blue bird toward the sun. It's a memorial to a baby who died and whose mother attended the school.*

PHOTO BY KATHERINE JONES

the Boise School District opened an accredited school at Booth for pregnant and parenting teens, offering grades 7 through 12, as it does today.

The availability of birth control and the decreasing stigma of unmarried pregnancies started to make homes and hospitals like Booth obsolete in the 1970s. Most closed

or, like Boise's, evolved. The rooms once devoted to labor and maternity became classrooms instead.

In 2002, the complex became the Marian Pritchett School at The Salvation Army Booth Memorial Campus, named in honor of Pritchett, a longtime teacher who died that same year.

Boise Main Auction

Things were rough in the Midwest in the Great Depression. So Paul Owens picked up, moved to Boise and founded the Boise Main Auction 75 years ago.

The first auction building was where the Shilo Inn sits now, said Owens descendant David Wesely Jr. He owns and operates the fourth-generation business today.

In the 1940s, the auction moved to its current home — an airy barnlike structure on Main Street. Auctions take place every Saturday morning.

The auction is prime for people-watching, whether you're bidding or not.

For one thing, there's the auctioneers' expert patter. An auctioneer extolled the virtues of a rusty wagon wheel: "Yuppies will pay top dollar for this kind of thing for their landscaping," he said, dragging out the syllables of the last word in such a way that it left no doubt about what he thought of yuppies and their landscaping.

Then there's the merchandise. Piles of stuff — ceramic horse-head vases, table lamps, 1980s-style nightstands, walkers, record albums. It all fills a series of bays in the auction barn. You can look through the chain-link fence to try to spot treasures. Some buyers come equipped with flashlights to see into the bays' dark recesses.

The auction runs on a consignment system. "John Doe brings in his items, we sell them, he takes home a percentage," said Wesely. "It runs pretty much how it always did."

Shelley Smith Eichmann, whose family has been in the Boise real estate business since the city's earliest days, nominated the Main Auction as a Boise icon, calling it a "local treasure."

When her real estate clients are moving and have items that they can't sell but that are too good to give away, she sends them to the Main Auction. "Sometimes what they earn is a disappointment. But sometimes it's amazing," said Eichmann.

Buyers, like sellers, love the thrill of the unknown, said Wesely. His customers range from people with a couple of bucks in their pockets to millionaires: "They all come down here looking for the good deal."

Shopping in a store is one thing. An auction is something else.

"Here you are participating in the action. We tease people. They have a good time. They get drawn in. It's a magnet," said Wesely.

DID YOU KNOW?

The auction's cafe has been around as long as the auction itself. Founder Paul Owens' wife, Grace, used to keep the cafe open every day. She baked pies most days. Today, it serves biscuits and gravy, the "farmer's platter" and "a little bit of everything," said David Wesely.

PHOTO BY
DARIN OSWALD

Beautiful Neon

What's your favorite piece of Boise neon?

The sign at the Torch Lounge casts a fiery glow onto Main Street. The nose-to-nose dragons at the Twin Dragon nearby have lured diners since the early 1960s. The Chinese characters spell the name of the restaurant in lights.

The blue and red sign at the Boise Rescue Mission has been a beacon for people in need for decades. When the mission moved its shelter from Front to 13th Street in 2006, it rehabbed its '70s-era neon and brought it along.

"It helped us tell people that even though we were moving from one building to another, our mission was the same," said Executive Director Bill Roscoe.

The sign Downtown at Dunkley

PHOTO BY KYLE GREEN

DID YOU KNOW? *Twin Dragon's neon includes simpler, but cool, red neon on the building's back wall as well.*

Music boasts bold, loopy, school penmanship-style neon. The Veltex sign still shines at 5th and Main, even though swank condos have replaced the service station that installed it.

The Boulevard Mo-Tel on Capitol Boulevard is low-income city hous-ing. But its 1938 neon sign, advertis-ing "TV" and "room telephones," earned a restoration grant in 1998 from the Idaho Heritage Trust.

Boisean Vangie Osborn created the Signs of Our Times project several years ago. She and other members of the group have collected old signs — neon, electric and others — that longtime Boiseans will remember. They include the cat's-eye sunglasses from Royal Optical (from 8th and Idaho), the sign from the Cub Tavern (now Bar Gernika), and the sign from Mel Day's Fiesta Ballroom that hung at 6th and Idaho in the 1960s — complete with pink maracas.

Many hope the signs, now in storage around the city, will end up in a display on the exterior back wall at the Idaho State Historical Museum. That project depends on money. Many of the signs require serious rehab and renovation. Osborn continues to collect them. She wants to fill the empty spaces on her group's wish list.

The holy grails of lost local signs? Fearless Farris, the Stinker Station skunk who waved his electrified tail at drivers on Front Street, and a giant woman's high heel that rotated

over King's Shoe Store near 8th and Idaho.

Osborn and others hope these treasures are stashed in a local garage somewhere and are not at the bottom of a landfill.

PHOTO BY DARIN OSWALD

DID YOU KNOW? *The wonderful neon at the Torch Lounge glows bright. Other signs are languishing. You can see the rusted, Deco-style Bouquet Bar sign stashed behind an outbuilding at the Old Pen.*

Cabana Inn's Red Hat

A list of the distinctive — some would say quirky — oversized objects that make up the Boise skyline includes the washer woman and giant diamond ring on Vista Avenue; the prancing white horse at Main and 6th; and the Spanish red bolero hat that for decades has floated over the Cabana Inn. It boasts the presence of RCA color TVs.

The Cabana Inn was built in 1971. Raja Patel bought it around 2003. He lives in a small apartment attached to the office.

A statuette of Ganesh, the elephant-headed Hindu deity, sits on the front desk. One recent afternoon, the office was filled with the aroma of home-cooked food.

Patel has fielded inquiries from

PHOTO BY ANNA WEBB

DID YOU KNOW? *The Cabana's red hat has other doppelgangers nearby besides Rick Friesen's mural. Artist Veronica Hollingshead painted a version of the hat on the hotel's back wall in 2010. A sign on Main Street not far from the hotel also pictures the famous hat and the words "Copa Cabana Inn." Stand in the middle of 16th Street and you can see three of the four hats at one time.*

people who want to buy the Cabana's iconic sign. They've offered thousands of dollars, said Patel. They've changed their minds when he's told them they would have to build him a new sign if they took the old one.

Patel hired artist Rick Friesen to

paint the mural on the hotel's east wall in 2007. Friesen took some artistic license and placed the bolero front and center.

"Drive through Boise, you can't really miss the Cabana's sign," Friesen said.

Flying Pie Pizzaria

Dave and Connie Parker founded Flying Pie in 1978, opening their flagship shop on Fairview when Jimmy Carter was president and "Annie Hall" won the best picture Oscar.

Flying Pie, with its counterculture sensibility, was a departure from the standard pizza of the time. Look no further than the logo painted on the shop's front wall: It's a knock-off from R. Crumb's "Keep on Truckin'" comic.

The restaurant's longtime owner, Howard Olivier, anticipated Boise tastes. He started importing kegs of beer before it became a common thing to do. He expanded the pizza operation. Flying Pie has three locations across the Valley. The restaurant also has a website with a timeline —

PHOTO BY KATHERINE JONES

DID YOU KNOW? *Howard Olivier and Flying Pie spearheaded the effort to install the exclamation mark — also a Boise icon — on the facade of the Boise Public Library.*

an oddity in itself.

That timeline includes genuinely strange things, such as delivering a pizza to Alaska; monitoring the expanding girth of a giant foil ball named Flora; and taking 62 employees and guests to Costa Rica for a week

thanks to a travel fund that began in a tip jar near the cash register.

Since 1984, Flying Pie has won more than 30 "best pizza" awards in various publications.

Florian Penalva bought Flying Pie in 2011.

Tin Pan Alley

Not everyone realizes that Boise has its own Tin Pan Alley, a tiny back lane that became a street.

The short road is tucked away in the middle of an odd-shaped block between 19th and 21st streets, just south of the Westside Drive-In on State Street.

As the story goes, a piano player who lived in one of the houses along the alley inspired the name. The Ada County Highway District installed a Tin Pan Alley street sign in 1992.

Boise's list of colorful street names includes Lovers Lane, which appeared on city maps between 1864 and 1921.

In later years, property owners petitioned the city to change the name to Pioneer Street, which still runs through the River Street neighborhood.

PHOTO BY ANNA WEBB

DID YOU KNOW? *The name Tin Pan Alley has its origins in a neighborhood in New York City around 28th Street between 5th Avenue and Broadway, where several music publishers kept their offices in the late 19th century. "Tin pan" refers to the clattering sound of lots of people sampling songs simultaneously on cheap pianos.*

According to the city's Arts and History Department, the lane's name had genuinely romantic origins. In 1864, when the city was just a year old, a young neighborhood woman named Ellen Hayes came down with typhoid fever. Dr. William Thompson nursed her back to health. The two fell in love, got married and had several children.

Finger Steaks

The truth about whether finger steaks were invented in Boise is one of those things that can never be proved. But, like the persistent rumor that Boise's underground supports a tangled web of Chinese tunnels, the story lives on. Finger steaks — deep-fried strips of battered meat — are Boise originals.

Some say The Torch Lounge was the first restaurant to serve them. Some say chef Mylo Bybee invented them before joining The Torch's kitchen staff in the late 1940s. Some say the original Torch owners invented them.

Whatever the truth, Idahoans' affection for the finger steak lives on. When Idaho was deciding on an image to adorn the state quarter, someone submitted a vote for the finger steak written on a cocktail

PHOTO BY KATHERINE JONES

DID YOU KNOW? *The Torch's awning once boasted "Home of the finger steak." The lounge has been reborn as a gentlemen's club. But diners can still find a good finger steak in town. In the Idaho Statesman's 2012 Best of Treasure Valley competition, readers gave the finger steaks at the Westside Drive-In top marks. Pictured here: finger steaks at O'Michael's Pub and Grill, another favorite.*

napkin. The peregrine falcon won out.

When it comes to condiments, one local insists that finger steaks must be served with cocktail sauce for the true Boise experience. Outside city limits, he was shocked to see that pretenders to the finger steak throne have adopted their own traditions. In Payette, his finger steaks arrived with a side of honey. Honey?

Albertsons Flagship Store

A monument in the corner of the parking lot reminds shoppers that Joe Albertson, founder of the supermarket chain, opened the store in the summer of 1939.

Billed in the news as "Idaho's largest and finest food store," it was huge — 10,000 square feet of shopping space, eight times the size of a typical store in 1939.

According to groceteria.com, a website that's devoted to the history of the supermarket industry, 75 cents bought three pounds of tomatoes, a pound of coffee and a one-pound roast.

The store offered never-before-seen attractions: an in-store bakery, fresh popcorn, roasted nuts, a doughnut machine and an ice cream

PHOTO PROVIDED BY ALBERTSONS

DID YOU KNOW? *Grocery founder Joe Albertson practiced a simple philosophy: "You've got to give the customer the merchandise they want, at a price they can afford, complete with lots of tender, loving care."*

shop offering the "Big Joe's" double cone for a nickel.

When Albertson opened his first store, there were only 25,000 residents in the city. Neighborhoods were dotted with small corner groceries,

the likes of the much-mourned Hollywood Market in the North End and the still operating Roosevelt Market in the East End. The "super" market was a whole new concept for Boiseans in the years just before World War II.

AAA Sign Co.

Paul Ashley opened the AAA Sign Co. with his brother, Art, in Boise's Hyde Park in 1944. Their father was a sign maker, too, said current proprietor Justinian Morton.

Before the Ashleys opened their business in the distinctive clapboard structure, it was a tinsmith's shop.

The building still has its original roof — sheet iron stamped with fish scale shingles. The roof's provenance is impressive: It came from the original territorial Capitol building that stood on the present-day Capitol Mall, said Morton.

The Ashleys represented a "modern wave" in signs, he said.

Their style, still visible around town at Riebe's Shoe Shop in Hyde Park and elsewhere, was simple and sleek. Paul Ashley drew the original Kuna Caveman mascot.

PHOTO BY ANNA WEBB

DID YOU KNOW? *Boise native Justinian Morton feels a kinship with Paul Ashley. The two have the same birthday: Jan. 11, more than 40 years apart. When Morton came on board as a partner at the now-closed Acme Vintage Clothing shop in Boise decades ago, Paul Ashley made the sign. It was one of his last.*

Ashley's flat file drawers filled with presentation drawings and photos of his work are in the shop where he left them. It's like a museum of sign craft — a document of the city, preserved in amber, said Morton.

When Morton was repainting the shop's exterior, a score of people stopped by, outraged that he was painting over the signs. Until they learned he was making them look as good as they did circa World War II.

"This place is as iconic as anything in Boise can be," he said.

Even as the city is changing, places such as AAA make it unique, said Morton. "This is something we have that is specific to Boise."

Hyde Park

The neighborhood, established in 1891, was among the first suburban developments outside the city's original Downtown core.

Around 1890, the year Idaho became a state, the city was in the midst of a building boom.

Investors platted several new subdivisions between 1890 and 1893, including Central Addition (near where Concordia Law School sits now), two subdivisions in South Boise (near where Boise State sits now) and four north of Fort Street, clustered around 13th Street: Brumback, Bryon, Lemp and Hyde Park.

The Boise Rapid Transit company laid tracks on 13th Street in 1893, spurring more settlement in the area. Thirteenth Street was unpaved at the time, but workers laid a strip of bricks and installed rails down

PHOTO BY DARIN OSWALD

DID YOU KNOW? *The neighborhood lost beloved longtime resident barber Vince Echevarria in 2012. He cut hair for 38 years on 13th Street.*

the middle of the street, said historian Barbara Perry Bauer, author of "Treasure Valley's Electric Railway."

The investors who platted the North End subdivisions intended from the beginning that their developments would be both residential

and commercial, said Perry Bauer.

The plan worked. The intersection of 13th and Eastman Street became a commercial hub, complete with an Odd Fellows Lodge and shops offering everything from dresses to freshly cut meat. Only South Boise had a neighborhood shopping area outside the city center equivalent to that of Hyde Park, say city historians. Hyde Park had a post office at 13th and Eastman and a newspaper oddly named the Hyde Park Radio that began publishing in 1923.

The origins of the Hyde Park name likely harked back to the Hyde Park neighborhood in London, said historian John Bertram. Eventually, the name caught on as the general name for the North 13th Street area.

Many of Hyde Park's historic buildings stand today. They include the Odd Fellows building at 1607 N. 13th St. It was built in 1902, the first two-story brick building in the neighborhood.

The Waymire Building at 1521 N. 13th was built in 1909. It's unique for being built entirely of cement bricks. The Waymires ran a grocery store on the ground floor and lived in apartments upstairs.

IDAHO STATESMAN FILE

DID YOU KNOW? *Tourtellotte and Hummel designed the 1907 Immanuel Methodist Episcopal Church in Hyde Park. The church is now home to the Treasure Valley Institute for Children's Arts. The organization is renovating the building. Before its reincarnation as an arts center, Preservation Idaho included the church on its list of the most endangered historic sites in the state.*

Longtime businesses include Riebe's Shoe Repair, which opened its first Boise store in 1906, moved to 13th Street in 1920 and is still open today.

In 1980, the city designated Hyde Park as a local historic district. In 1982, it was listed in the National Register of Historic Places.

Camel's Back

Joe Vitley, who turned 79 in the city's sesquicentennial year, is a North End native. He went to Washington Elementary, graduated from Boise State University and had a career in the military and civil service. When he was a boy, he spent his time on Camel's Back hill.

Winter meant sledding, even a little skiing.

"We had more snow back then. On a moonlit night, you could go up the hill and sleigh ride until you froze to death. And sometimes you did. But it was a beautiful experience," Vitley said.

He nominated Camel's Back hill as a Boise icon.

In the summer, Vitley and his friends found lizards, horned toads and "a snake or two."

"It was wild and woolly back then," he said.

Anytime the neighborhood kids found an old car fender, they carried it to the top of the hill and rode it down, skimming through the weeds.

Vitley once watched his cousin walk down Camel's Back wearing stilts. "I don't know how he did it, but I saw it. That boy lived on the edge."

Vitley credits a young man from the neighborhood with cutting the hill's first trails with his motorcycle in the 1940s.

"We called him Blackie because he had a black motorcycle and wore a black suit," said Vitley.

Blackie and his fellow riders tore up the front side of the hill, known by neighborhood kids as the "angel slide." They careened down its back, known as the "devil slide."

Angel or devil, the whole hill was a playground.

"We killed buffalo, played cowboys and Indians on that hill, and dug foxholes to fight the Germans," he said.

His grandchildren play on Camel's Back now. The foxholes are still there.

DID YOU KNOW? *Boisean Bernard Lemp sold the Camel's Back property to the city in 1932. Camel's Back was dedicated as a city park in 1965. The National Guard, the Rotary and Optimist clubs, and the Boise Jaycees all helped pay for park amenities. The park covers 11 acres and connects to the Ridge to Rivers trail system.*

IDAHO STATESMAN FILE

Harrison Boulevard

Boise's boulevard, bisected by a row of shade trees, possesses undeniable grandiosity — in its scale, in the stone lions that guard 1505, in the columns and triangular pediment at 1201, or even in the cool, white Art Moderne hipness of 1717, a house that feels no compunction about its lack of style similarities with its neighbors.

Once known as 17th Street, it became Harrison Boulevard in 1891 after President Benjamin Harrison visited Boise. Harrison signed the Admissions Act that made Idaho the 43rd state on July 3, 1890.

An advertisement for life on the boulevard appeared in the Idaho Statesman in 1894.

"The only genuinely pleasant drive in Boise is Harrison Boulevard, 100 feet wide and one mile long," it read.

IDAHO STATESMAN FILE PHOTOS

DID YOU KNOW? *Harrison Boulevard got its street lamps and its distinctive median parkway in 1916. The city engineer called Harrison Boulevard a "model road."*

"If the beautiful pleases you, nobody else is in it."

Harrison was sure to be one of the "bon-ton," or fashionable residence

sites in the city, claimed the ad.

Boiseans started moving there in larger numbers after 1901.

Despite its scale and presidential moniker, Harrison Boulevard isn't all about grandiosity, said Dan Everhart of Preservation Idaho.

"While we do think of Harrison as a place where Boise's elite have lived, there's also a history of Harrison being a democratic place. It's hard to shoehorn the neighborhood into a single class structure."

What it lacked in ethnic diversity, the boulevard possessed in economic diversity. Harrison was home to doctors, lawyers, merchants and politicians, but it also had more modest homes on smaller lots.

Old records, for instance, show that through the years, 900 Harrison was home to salesmen, musicians, a bartender and a teacher, among others.

"There was always an interesting social mix on Harrison, and there still is," Everhart said.

Boise Co-op

A few dozen locals founded the Boise Co-op in 1973 as a food-buying club. The philosophy was getting good, bulk food and selling it to members at a discount. The co-op's first home was a back room at the El-Ada community outreach center.

In 1975, the co-op moved to a storefront in Hyde Park, the former home of the Salvation Army. In this era, members had to put in hours at the store to get their member discounts, said Dave Kirkpatrick, a long-time employee. A space on Hill Road, not far from Harrison Boulevard, was the co-op's next stop in 1984.

Kirkpatrick credits then-leader Ken Kavanagh with the co-op's shift in philosophy. This was an era when "organic" wasn't yet a buzzword, when "foodie" wasn't yet a movement, when gluten was not public

PHOTO BY ANNA WEBB

DID YOU KNOW? *When the co-op moved into the former M&W Market, the city asked the store to incorporate the old market sign into a new, structural piece. The co-op hired artist Chris Binion to create "Boxfall" in 1998 — a nod to grocery boxes.*

enemy No. 1, and when the idea of televised cooking competitions would have seemed like something from "Monty Python." But the co-op was in the right place at the right time, anticipating the community's embrace of food as an art form. The

co-op began seeking out products such as Italian canned tomatoes and high-end olive oil. Indian spices. Beer and wine. And meat. Some liked the changes, some didn't. Membership evolved.

"Todd Giesler (another longtime employee) got it right," said Kirkpatrick. "We had tie-dye and VW vans in the morning, Versace and Lexuses in the afternoon."

In the 1980s, the co-op started to raise money for its building program. Rick Troyer was the first member to invest in the new program. He received card No. 1. The card turns heads when he shops and the checkout person asks for his membership number. "I usually just hand over my card," he said. "It's more fun to watch their expressions."

The co-op moved to its current location, the former M&W Market, in 1996. The co-op had more than 22,000 active members in 2013.

Jim's Rooster

Thanks to a naming contest at St. Joseph's Catholic School, the giant rooster on the roof of Jim's Coffee Shop on Fort Street has a name: Rudy.

Name or no name, the bird has stood proud, his chest puffed out over Fort Street, for decades. Rudy is 7 feet tall. He's made of fiberglass and weighs about 100 pounds.

The bird's origins are a little mysterious, said Dave Fellows, who bought the business in 1983.

A longtime barber named Jerry used to cut hair in the shop next to Jim's. Jerry told Fellows that the cafe's former owner, Al Landers, bought Rudy from a traveling salesman in the 1960s.

The visuals for this version of the story are fantastic. Sure, chances are any giant bird would have been

IDAHO STATESMAN FILE

DID YOU KNOW? *Contrary to rumor, pranksters have never stolen the bird. "But he has been graffitied," said owner Dave Fellows. "I've had to go up there and scrub him down."*

paid for and delivered by freight at a later date. But it's impossible to not imagine a salesman driving across the West, clean dress shirts swaying in his back seat and Rudy strapped to the top of his car.

As it happens, the traveling salesman tale is pure urban legend.

Jim Montgomery, the cafe's namesake, bought the business

from Landers in 1971. Landers, Montgomery said, bought Rudy from Merrill Egg Farm in Eagle in the 1960s.

In any case, the bird has always attracted attention.

"I meet people. I tell them I'm Jim of Jim's Coffee Shop. They talk about the rooster," said Montgomery.

Chapter Four EAST BOISE/DOWNTOWN

Rainbow Trout

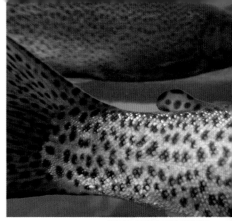

PHOTO BY PETE ZIMOWSKY

The population of rainbow trout in the Boise River was healthy in 2013, more than twice what it was a decade earlier, said Andy Brunelle, an officer in the local Ted Trueblood chapter of Trout Unlimited. That's thanks to higher winter water flows, protection of riparian areas, habitat restoration and fishing regulations, said Brunelle.

The Idaho Department of Fish and Game counts fish in a few sections of the Boise River every three years. In 1994, there were 288 wild rainbow trout in a one-mile stretch. In 2010, there were 5,116.

Brunelle nominated the native rainbow, known for its spots and iridescent scales, as a Boise icon.

"You know as well as I the image of the fly angler standing in the Boise River with the city buildings in the background," said Brunelle.

"It would not be a legitimate image were it not for the trout that have re-established in the past decades after they were pretty much wiped out."

The nadir for trout in the Boise followed the construction of Lucky Peak Dam in the mid-1950s. The dam blocked winter flows from Mores Creek, Brunelle said.

In that era — one that preceded Boise's embrace of its river — pollution also harmed the trout. The river was a dump site for industrial waste and sewer discharges. What little water there was, was dirty. Establishment of the Greenbelt in the early 1970s, coupled with federal clean water regulations, helped the fish recover. Agencies also worked to increase winter water levels in the

DID YOU KNOW? *Rainbow trout are not free of controversy. In "An Entirely Synthetic Fish: How Rainbow Trout Beguiled America and Overran the World," writer Anders Halverson says agencies have stocked rainbows in every state and on every continent except Antarctica, sometimes to the detriment of native species.*

Boise River.

High winter flows mean more shallow channels where young trout can shelter, as well as bigger breeding grounds for the insects trout eat.

Bonneville Point

While technically not in Boise, Bonneville Point may be the ultimate Boise icon.

A local legend claims a hunting party led by explorer Benjamin Bonneville arrived at this spot on a desert bluff east of Boise in 1833.

The travelers saw the green, cottonwood-filled valley before them after their long trek through the sagebrush and delighted, "The woods, the woods!" in French.

As most Boise elementary students learn, "les bois" morphed into "Boise."

The Bonneville story has its detractors, including those who claim earlier explorers used similar French terms for the area long before Bonneville. Annie Laurie Bird, author of "Boise, The Peace Valley," called it a tall tale.

Still, the legend lives on. It is, at

DID YOU KNOW? *Benjamin Bonneville crossed Idaho several times along an old Indian trail that became the Oregon Trail through the Boise Valley. Today, Bonneville Point is a small park with interpretive signs. Walking trails follow old wagon ruts.*

this point, as integral to the founding of the city as anything else.

Washington Irving, familiar as the author of "The Legend of Sleepy Hollow," wrote "The Adventures of Captain Bonneville" in 1837.

Irving included Bonneville's thoughts about the Boise area.

"The country about the Boisee (or Woody) River is extolled by Captain Bonneville as the most enchanting he had seen in the Far West, presenting the mingled grandeur and beauty of mountain and plain, of bright running streams and vast grassy meadows waiving to the breeze."

Foote Homesite

Mining engineer Arthur Foote, a transplant from Connecticut, was the first to envision a system of canals and dams that would bring water from the Boise Canyon to farms in the 1880s.

In those days, the federal government didn't fund irrigation projects, so Foote found private investors. He laid the groundwork for an irrigation system, but the project ran out of money.

Twenty-five years and many setbacks later, the system Foote imagined became a reality after the Reclamation Act of 1902 provided funding for Arrowrock and Diversion dams.

Foote, in the meantime, had left Idaho for California, convinced that his project was a failure.

Writer and illustrator Mary Hallock Foote, Arthur's wife, wrote

IDAHO STATESMAN FILE PHOTOS

DID YOU KNOW? *Writer Wallace Stegner loosely based his book "Angle of Repose" on the life of Mary Hallock Foote. It's partly set in early-day Boise. At right, the canyon and Boise River near the Foote homesite.*

about their Idaho travails in her memoir, "A Victorian Gentlewoman in the Far West."

During their time in the area, the Footes lived in a stone house near Lucky Peak. The house is long gone. There's not much left to see besides a few stones from the foundation. The area is mostly popular with dog-walkers and bird-watchers.

Understated as it is, the old site represents a key chapter in the long, frequently tempestuous story of moving water around the West.

The old homesite is in Foote Park at the base of Lucky Peak Dam on the south side of the river, across from Discovery Park. A split-rail fence and small interpretive signs mark where the house stood.

Lucky Peak Dam

If you grew up in Boise, there's a fair chance you've said or heard the words, "Let's go to Lucky Peak," about a million times.

The site of school field trips and family outings, the Lucky Peak complex on Idaho 21 includes the dam, a lake, a power plant, more than 4,000 acres of public lands and Sandy Point, a little beach with its own fountainlike aeration spout.

The curve of Sandy Point is the natural curve of the river.

"If the dam were not there, the bend would still be there," said Joyce Dunning, operations manager for the Army Corps of Engineers at Lucky Peak.

The corps began building Lucky Peak in 1949 — a few years after Congress authorized the Flood Control Act of 1946. The dam

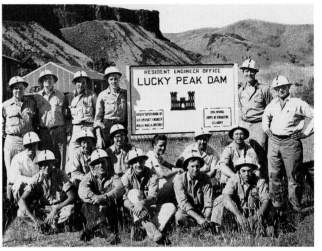

DID YOU KNOW?

Lucky Peak is a "rolled earthfill" dam. Engineers found an anchor of solid bedrock, dynamited to reach it, and began building the dam with dirt and rocks. At left, the Lucky Peak building crew, circa 1950.

PHOTO PROVIDED BY THE ARMY CORPS OF ENGINEERS

opened in June 1955 to much fanfare, said Dunning.

The dam is about 250 feet tall. Flood control and irrigation make the water levels in the lake fluctuate by as much as 150 feet — hence the chalky horizontal lines visible on the slopes down to the water.

Lucky Peak's name harks back to the gold rush days of the 1860s, said Dunning. Prospectors identified a couple of spots where they thought they might find the precious metal. They found it on Shaw Mountain on an outcropping that came to be called Lucky Peak.

As the story goes, there was an "Unlucky Peak" as well, where prospectors weren't so fortunate. Dunning has yet to find that peak on a map.

DID YOU KNOW?

The 150-foot "rooster tail" at Lucky Peak Dam is an icon within an icon. Engineers intended the rooster tail to dissipate the pressure of the water as it flows through the dam. The corps opened a power plant in 1988 and started harnessing the pressurized water to generate electricity. The rooster tail is a special occasion these days, allowed to spew only when there is an excess of water in the local dam system.

PHOTO BY DARIN OSWALD

195

Oregon Trail

For lots of communities in the U.S., the idea of the Oregon Trail is just that — an idea, an abstraction that lives in textbooks and movies.

But for Boiseans, the Oregon Trail is a tangible thing. It's often no more than a few blocks away from where you're standing. It often corresponds to a road you walk or drive every day.

Over a 20-year period beginning around 1841, around 300,000 people traveled the trail on their way to Oregon.

The route enters Boise east of town, past trail ruts preserved at the Oregon Trail Reserve on East Lake Forest Drive. It passes near the Bown House on ParkCenter Boulevard and continues on through South Boise.

It crosses the Oregon Trail Memorial Bridge on Capitol Boule-vard, the spot where ferries carried passengers across the river. It heads into Downtown Boise. It continues through town and the North End. It passes close to the Idaho State Capitol and the O'Farrell Cabin (Boise's first house) at 5th and Fort before heading west, out of town along Hill Road.

Twenty-one obelisks help mark the route, thanks to an effort that began in the 1990s in South Boise Village, the neighborhood south of Boise Avenue.

Glen Corbeil was part of a local effort to beautify Boise Avenue, which follows the Oregon Trail route. Corbeil applied for neighborhood and federal grants. Public artist Mark Baltes joined Corbeil and added more markers in the North End.

Each marker includes an interpre-tive plaque about a different aspect of local history.

The Idaho Statesman lauded the effort in a 2004 editorial:

"It has taken 10 years, but the obelisks are here to stay. Boise owes a debt of gratitude to Corbeil, Baltes and other local residents who built them. Their work has improved neighborhoods, fostered appreciation for history and enriched our city."

Here is a sampling of marker locations and themes: Protest Avenue and Boise Avenue-Farming in Boise; Rossi Avenue and Boise Avenue-Black Pioneers; Euclid Avenue and Boise Avenue-Table Rock; McAuley Park at Harrison Boulevard and Hays Street-Emigrant Trails to Goodales Cutoff; Dewey Park at 15th Street and Hill Road-Slaugh-terhouse Gulch.

DID YOU KNOW? *The 2,170-mile-long Oregon Trail stretched from Independence, Mo., to Oregon City, Ore. To travel the entire length took five months. The trail passes through Missouri, Kansas, Nebraska, Wyoming, Idaho and Oregon. In Boise, the trail became Main Street in the city's first 10 blocks that pioneers platted in 1863. Pictured here: the trail east of Boise.*

Idaho Shakespeare Festival Amphitheater

Because of this amphitheater, all of the following are possible in a single evening: smelling cottonwood trees while listening to the words of the Bard and the honks of geese; starting your evening with a picnic while it's 100 degrees outside and ending it with a sweater and a thermos of hot chocolate; watching the sunlight dim on the Foothills as the lights get brighter on the stage.

The Idaho Shakespeare Festival presented plays for 20 years before the amphitheater opened as its permanent home in 1998.

On the bill for the venue's first season: "A Midsummer Night's Dream," "Romeo and Juliet" and "Cymbeline."

It took three years to find the perfect spot for the amphitheater, said Mark Hofflund, the festival's managing director. Festival leaders considered 40 sites, including Warm Springs Community Park behind Adams Elementary and Veterans Memorial State Park. None of them worked out.

When the Idaho Foundation for Parks and Lands suggested its land on the far end of Warm Springs, festival leaders got inspired. They saw the beauty of the place — the light, the trees, the location beside the 480-acre Barber Pool Conservation Area. The area is home to one of the largest stands of native black cottonwood trees in the region, not to mention 200 species of wildlife, Hofflund said.

A private/public partnership among the festival, the Idaho Department of Parks and Recreation and the Idaho Foundation for Parks and Lands secured the land for the amphitheater. The partners kicked off a capital campaign to build it in 1997.

The design of the amphitheater harks back to the circular Globe Theater in London built by Shakespeare's acting company, Hofflund said.

The classical amphitheaters of Greece and Rome also influenced the design.

Lead theater architect Gene Angell began his career as a scenic designer for the stage. The amphitheater's placement with a dramatic Foothills backdrop was intentional.

"When people come to a play for the first time, they tell me they've never realized the Foothills were so beautiful until they saw them with the sun setting, framed by the stage," Hofflund said.

DID YOU KNOW? *Some of the amphitheater's sandstone came from the Odd Fellows Building that once stood on 9th Street (where Berryhill & Co. is now). The complex also includes about 200 tons of donated sandstone from the city's Sand Creek drainage flume.*

Boise River

The Boise River is, in a word, "fabulous," said Dave Cannamela, superintendent of the MK Nature Center.

"Even with man's intervention, the dams, the changing hydrology, the river still brings joy. It makes you feel good," he said.

The Boise originates in the high reaches of the Sawtooth Range. It flows west through the heart of Boise, connecting to the Snake River near Parma.

For Cannamela, the size of the river is key. It's not huge like the Columbia, where you stand on the shore and just feel its awesomeness.

"You wade into the Boise, you're in view of the other shore," said Cannamela.

The Boise is a river with a human scale. It supports all kinds of life, from river otters to yellow-headed and red-winged blackbirds.

Screech owls nest in the native cottonwoods on its shores.

Rainbow and brown trout, mountain whitefish, bottom-dwelling sculpins and native suckers live in the Boise, said Cannamela.

"Nobody gives a sucker an even break," he quipped. But even the creature with the nonromantic name belongs. "Everybody plays a part," he said. "Suckers are the vacuum cleaners."

The Boise's currents move the rich sediment where cottonwood seeds — carried in distinctive white tufts — take hold and grow.

Most Boiseans have a memory of the river. For Scott Smith, who grew up in Boise, it was foraging for empty beer and pop cans when he was in junior high. He and his friends wanted to recycle the cans to buy gear to climb Table Rock quarry.

They'd venture out on busy float weekends. Enlisting one of their dad's rafts, they'd float until they came to spots where they knew cans collected.

"My favorite was a giant eddy just below one of the three falls," said Smith.

"The contents of all those spilled coolers would get caught in that eddy."

The boys would put on masks and flippers and dive in.

"In the strange underwater soundscape, we'd hear the cans before we saw them, clanking and bumping. Then, out of the green gloom, a dense school of cans emerged, swarming and swirling," Smith recalled.

"We'd grab as many as we could, kick up to the surface, toss them into the raft, then dive again."

There were rewards in addition to the money they got from recycling. Sometimes the cans were full. The boys drank the pop and gave the beer to their folks.

"And when floaters realized what we were up to, they were genuinely surprised and grateful for our 'good deed,'" said Smith.

DID YOU KNOW? *The Boise has been known by other names through the centuries. Explorer Robert Stuart called it "The Wooded River" as early as 1812. British fur traders continued to use the name, but also called the Boise Reid's River for trader John Reid, who established a post near the river in 1813.*

PHOTO BY DARIN OSWALD

Bown House

Pioneer Joseph Bown came to Idaho from Iowa in 1862, drawn by the promise of finding gold. In addition to that quest, he began farming near the Boise River and what's now ParkCenter Boulevard.

In 1865, when the city of Boise was just a couple of years old, Bown went back to Iowa and returned with his wife, Temperance, and their five young children. He built the family's sandstone house, originally called the "block house" because of its distinctive shape, in 1879.

Statesman reader Juno Van Ocker, a retired teacher from the Boise School District, nominated the historic house as her favorite Boise icon. Van Ocker is a volunteer docent at the site. She shared some of its history.

The Bowns built the house, made

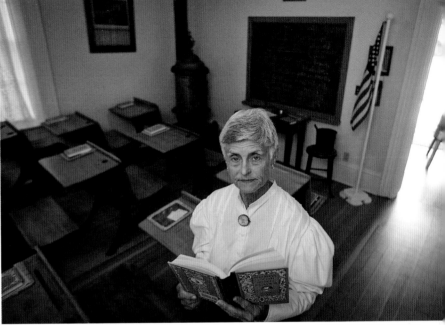

PHOTOS BY DARIN OSWALD

Juno Van Ocker's volunteer work at the Bown House includes dressing the part as a resident of territorial Idaho. The house sits next to the old Oregon Trail route. Immigrant diaries mention it.

of two colors of sandstone from local quarries, on the highest piece of land in the area. Their fellow Boiseans considered the house and its surrounding 240-acre farm large and luxurious.

The Boise School District owns the Bown House today, thanks to voters' approval of a 1987 bond. The district initially considered demolishing or moving the house to another site. Instead, the Idaho Historic Preservation Council (which became Preservation Idaho) convinced the district to keep it and find an educational use for it.

Local groups and individuals helped raise money to restore the house and grounds.

Today, the Bown House is part of the campus of Riverside School. It's home to the Heritage Education Program that lets students experience what life was like in the 1880s. The Assistance League of Boise, the school district and community donations support the program.

After the Bowns, a succession of families occupied the house until the late 1980s. The attic stairwell is covered in messages left by past residents. One proclaims affection for "Oklahoman singing cowboy Gene Autry."

The Murphy family raised 14 children in the house in the 1930s and 1940s. Mrs. Murphy carefully recorded their names and ages on the stairwell wall. Youngest was Larry DeWayne, described as the "baby of the family." After Larry was Allen Lee, described as "next to the baby" at 5 years old.

Van Ocker met some of the Murphy siblings when they returned to tour the house many years later as senior citizens. She asked them if the house had electricity when they lived there.

"They said they thought that it did, but that they were so poor they wouldn't have been able to afford to use it anyway," recalled Van Ocker.

The most recent stairwell inscription is from 1988. It's a plea from Carol Kersting, the Bown House's last resident. She asks that someone care for the house after she's gone. Before she died, Kersting got to see the house restored.

DID YOU KNOW? *In 1995, the Bown House won a National Preservation Honor Award from the National Trust, one of 15 given in the U.S. that year.*

"She left this world knowing it's in good hands," said Van Ocker.

Table Rock

Table Rock, one of the most familiar landscapes in the city, is really several icons in one.

First, there's the geology. The flat formation off Old Penitentiary Road is dotted with small caves and tiny crevasses along its slopes. It stands more than 3,600 feet high.

Table Rock owes its existence to Lake Idaho, the giant body of water that stretched from the Owyhees to Weiser, and from the Boise Front to Hagerman, around 5 million years ago.

Geologists say collections of fine lake sand formed Table Rock's distinct ledge-like shape. Geothermal springs cemented it into sandstone.

Lake Idaho eventually drained away through Hells Canyon, leaving behind notable formations such as Table Rock.

Human beings have interacted with Table Rock in many ways. Shoshone tribal members used the rock as a lookout. In the years shortly after pioneers platted the city of Boise in 1863, residents began flocking to the geothermal waters of Kelly Hot Springs, just east of Table Rock's slopes.

Table Rock was the source of the sandstone that built some of Boise's first structures, including the Old Pen.

Table Rock's "human-built environment" provides even more mini-icons.

In 1931, Boisean Ward Rolfe and a group of his friends from Boise High School drove a Model T Ford up the hill the year they graduated and formed a giant letter "B" out of rocks on Table Rock's southern slope.

"We decided Boise needed a B. So we went up there and put it up there," Rolfe told the Idaho Statesman in a 2006 interview.

Rolfe died in 2011 at the age of 100, but the B remains — painted and repainted in the colors of high schools from across the Valley.

The cross on Table Rock is also an icon. Like Boise's Ten Commandments monument — installed by the Eagles at the time of the popular "Ten Commandments" film — the Table Rock cross has its roots in 1950s popular culture.

Boisean Glenn Lungren, a member of the Jaycees service club, saw an episode of "This is Your Life" on television about a mail carrier who built a cross in his town.

Inspired, Lungren kicked off a drive to raise money for a similar cross in Boise. The drive succeeded and the Jaycees built the 60-foot cross in 1956 on Department of Correction land.

In the 1970s, in response to questions about a religious symbol on public property, the Department of Lands sold the .071 acre where the cross sits to the Jaycees for $100.

Over the next decades, the cross continued to be a lightning rod for opposing groups.

Standing on Table Rock amidst broadcast antennas, it inspired marches to the Capitol and letters to the editor from fans and detractors alike.

Some wish it gone. Some moved to Boise because they fell in love with it. Some see it as a beacon of faith, others as nothing more significant than a familiar light on the hill.

PHOTO BY KYLE GREEN

DID YOU KNOW? *Table Rock's close relationship to the capital city continues to grow and evolve. The area is part of the Ridge to Rivers trail system. Five Ridge to Rivers trails crisscross the area. Table Rock is also a spot to see wildflowers in the late spring, including arrowleaf balsam root, native pink phlox, wild rose and many more. Pictured here: the sesquicentennial "super moon" over Table Rock on June 22, 2013. A super moon occurs about once every 14 months when the moon makes its closest approach to earth.*

Bitterbrush

Bitterbrush, native to the hills around Boise, is a gnarly, medium-sized shrub. Its tiny pale yellow flowers look like miniature wild roses. This is appropriate because bitterbrush — Purshia tridentata in formal circles — is a member of the rose family. This might also have something to do with its exquisite fragrance.

"Their annual bloom fills the air with sweet perfume," said reader Christopher Trollan, who nominated bitterbrush as a Boise icon. "My wife says it's like a small perfume forest."

Bitterbrush is a key winter food source for deer, elk and antelope. The Idaho Department of Fish and Game recruits volunteers to plant bitterbrush, along with sagebrush, early each spring.

Rodents eat bitterbrush seeds, sometimes eating a plant's whole seed production for the season. Luckily, bitterbrush has remarkable regenerative properties. It can sprout roots where branches touch the ground and produce new plants.

Lewis and Clark collected bitterbrush in Montana in 1806. The plant's botanical name honors Frederick Pursh, the botanist who was the first to classify many of the Western specimens the explorers collected.

"Tridentata" means three-toothed, a leaf trait bitterbrush shares with sagebrush.

Find bitterbrush in the Foothills around Boise in the same places you find sagebrush and arrowleaf balsam root. Its range extends from the Cascades east to Montana and Colorado, and south to New Mexico.

PHOTO BY ANNA WEBB

DID YOU KNOW? *Native tribes made a purple dye from the seed coat of bitterbrush, and diapers and shoes from its bark.*

Sagebrush

Grow up in Boise and there's a good chance you'll develop a deep affection for — some would say addiction to — the aroma of sagebrush. That dusty, woody scent is emblematic of Boise and its Foothills.

Writer Mark Twain was of two minds about the West's native perfume.

"When crushed, sagebrush emits an odor which isn't exactly magnolia and equally isn't exactly polecat, but it is a sort of compromise between the two," he wrote to his wife from Nevada in 1861.

American Indians, including the Shoshone, used sagebrush as a cure for colds, stomachaches and fevers. A poultice of crushed leaves on the forehead cured headaches.

Settlers in the southern part of the state used big sage for Christmas

IDAHO STATESMAN FILE

DID YOU KNOW? *Cort Conley's book "Idaho for the Curious" includes more sage lore, including the story of an Emmett farmer who figured out how to graft gooseberry and currant stock to sagebrush roots.*

trees.

Artemisia tridentata is sagebrush's botanical name. Artemisia refers to Artemis, Greek goddess of the hunt and wilderness, said Cort Conley, director of literature at the Idaho Commission on the Arts.

"There's a whole saga about shampoo being made from sagebrush, sold to tourists as a tonic for baldness,"

said Conley.

The Sage Brush Tonic Co. in Shoshone sold such a product at the turn of the century. "Nature's own remedy for falling hair," boasted the company's advertisements.

Sagebrush is a critical habitat for wildlife, especially the sage grouse. Sagebrush can account for the birds' entire winter food source, said Conley.

The charms of Artemisia tridentata have not been lost on artists.

The Idaho State Historical Museum owns "The Sage Gatherers," a large oil painting by Joseph Patrick McMeekin, who lived and painted in the Hagerman canyon around 1910. The painting shows settlers collecting sagebrush for firewood.

The piece is "sort of an Idaho Millet painting," said Conley, referring to Jean-Francois Millet, a French painter known for his agrarian landscapes.

Sandstone

Consider historic structures in Boise and you'll hear three words again and again.

Two are "Tourtellotte" and "Hummel," principals of the architectural firm that arguably influenced the Boise skyline more than anyone.

The third: sandstone.

It's all around us — in the thick Romanesque walls of St. John's Cathedral, in tombstones in local cemeteries, in foundations of homes in Boise's oldest neighborhoods.

In 1899, city leaders approved an ordinance to install concrete sidewalks with "hard, heavy sandstone" curbs throughout the city. Some of those curbs remain, particularly on Main Street between 1st and 3rd near the Old Assay Office.

An interpretive sign on the Assay Office grounds includes a map of all the city's existing sandstone curbs.

Boise sandstone is everywhere in the surrounding natural world, too. When you walk in the Foothills, many of the prominent landforms you see are sandstone, said Sam Matson, a lecturer in Boise State's Department of Geosciences.

To understand the origins of local sandstone, start 5 million years ago, when the Treasure Valley was covered in water.

Lake Idaho — about 100 feet deep at its deepest point, a mud bog at its shallowest — stretched from the Owyhees to present-day Weiser, from the Boise Front on its northern edge to Hagerman in the east.

To get a sense of what that looked like, take a drive up Bogus Basin Road during a heavy inversion. The cloud layer replicates the edge of the lake, with just the Owyhees and the Boise Front visible above the clouds, said Matson.

The mountainous shores of Lake Idaho were made of granite. The lake lapped at the granite and broke it down into sand. That sand, pressed in a soup of groundwater and minerals, became sandstone.

In some places around Boise, including Hulls Gulch and Military Reserve, the sandstone is so soft and crumbly, officials post signs to warn people away for their own safety.

The sandstone from Table Rock is different, said Matson.

Geothermal water there broke down silica in volcanic rock to create an especially hard stone that's ideal for building — as Boise's century-old structures can attest.

Matson urges people to look closely at sandstone next time they're in the Foothills. The rocks tell stories, he said.

"The fossils, little ripples, all the evidence of this being the margin of a lake. They help one have a sense of place," he said.

DID YOU KNOW? *If you look closely at sandstone, you can often see telltale signs of its granite origins, including flakes of mica. Boise sandstone was often exported outside the city. Gothic buildings at Yale University in New Haven, Conn., as well as buildings in other cities, contain Boise sandstone.*

PHOTO BY
ANNA WEBB

Old Pen

The Idaho Territory built its first prison in 1870, 20 years before Idaho became a state. At the time, Boiseans considered the location at the foot of Table Rock — a former Shoshone lookout — remote.

No one anticipated that Boiseans would begin drilling for geothermal water near the prison in 1890, kicking off an era of residential development along Warm Springs Avenue.

Like other territorial-era buildings, including the Assay Office on Main Street and the structures at Fort Boise, the original territorial cell house at the Old Pen was built of local sandstone using federal design specifications.

The first 11 inmates arrived in 1872 from the Boise County Jail in Idaho City. Guards put them to work cutting sandstone in the quarry

PHOTO BY AMBER BEIERLE, OLD PENITENTIARY

DID YOU KNOW? *The prison's oldest building is the original territorial cell house. Converted to a chapel in the 1930s and burned in the 1970s, it once held 42 cells.*

nearby to construct more prison buildings.

Officials condemned the original cell house in the 1930s. A Works Progress Administration project converted it into a chapel.

By the early 1970s, plans were underway to move inmates to a new, larger prison south of the city. A riot at the Old Pen in 1973 hastened the move.

Prisoners burned the original cell house/chapel building in the riot. It still stands, but today is a roofless shell.

The prison, which the Idaho State Historical Society converted into a museum in the mid-1970s, includes a 69-grave cemetery on a slope outside the prison walls. Amber Beierle, interpretive specialist at the Old Pen, shared a few stories about the inmates buried there.

A court sentenced Rufus Roy Liggins to five to 10 years in the 1950s for writing a bad $20 check. Liggins was a Purple Heart veteran who served in World War II. He died in prison from the effects of his war wounds. A military headstone marks his grave.

One convicted robber, William Trent, escaped in 1880. He was injured in a shootout with guards and cavalry officers dispatched from Fort Boise to find him. Trent ended up in the prison infirmary, where he revealed that he was from a prominent East Coast family. When he died from his injuries, his family paid to erect one of the most elaborate stones in the cemetery.

Another notable grave is a monolith with the inscription "In memory of Bud Ray."

Police arrested Ray, 18, as he was riding a horse stolen from a rancher in Blackfoot. Ray got a two-year sentence for grand larceny. He died of a heart ailment in 1897, nine months into his sentence.

Raymond Snowden, convicted of murdering a woman in Garden City, was the last man hanged at the Old Pen, in 1957. He's buried on the hillside, but records are vague about the exact location.

Beierle said she's always intrigued by what draws the prison's many visitors to the site.

"We have those interested in the paranormal and the macabre," said Beierle. Others come to see "bonus" exhibitions, such as one dedicated to the Morrison Knudsen employees taken as prisoners of war on Wake Island during World War II. Another attraction: the J. Curtis Earle arms collection. Yes, there is a Gatling gun with a wagon mount dating to the 1860s. Yes, there is a sword from India that dates to the 9th century.

Even visitors without a particular agenda step back in time to get a clearer picture of how the West dealt with criminals.

Some inmates had the misfortune of spending time in solitary confinement, or "Siberia." Bare, unheated cells have tiny holes for light in the ceiling. One cell has a chilling bit of graffiti etched into its wall: "Every man has to walk a road right to the end and this is the end by God."

Bishops' House

The Bishops' House — a Queen Anne-style structure that sits among its sandstone companions at the Old Pen complex — represents the power of community and preservation.

The house was in danger of being torn down in 1975. A group called The Friends of the Bishops' House raised money to move it from the corner of Idaho and 2nd streets to Old Penitentiary Road and restore it.

Their efforts paid off with an Orchid Award from Preservation Idaho in 1981. Today, the house is available to rent for special events.

The Episcopal Church built the house in 1889 as a rectory for clergy.

Ten years later, the newly appointed Episcopal Bishop James Funsten hired architect James Tourtellotte to remodel it.

Tourtellotte transformed the residence into the Queen Anne mansion we know today. He added a parlor, living room, study, maid's room and guest rooms. According to the Statesman at the time, no trace of the original building remained after Tourtellotte's upgrades.

Boisean Rick Poplack, a member of the Bishops' House board, has researched the house's history.

Poplack found documents revealing that the 1899 remodel cost more than $7,000 — almost three and a half times what Funsten paid for the original house and land a decade earlier.

A series of bishops lived in the house until 1972. Its move in the mid-'70s turned up more curiosities, in addition to the claim that someone once saw a ghost on the house's staircase.

Ron Thurber, a retired preservation architect in Boise (who helped save the organ at the Egyptian), said preservationists found masses of ham radio antenna wire in the attic. Apparently one of the resident bishops — it's unclear which one — had been a ham radio operator when he lived there. He left the wire but not the radio.

Another curious fact: When movers transported the house from Downtown, the stone mason numbered the sandstone blocks so that builders could replace them in the correct order. The numbering plan went awry. Visitors, said Poplack, can see some of the stones in place, numbered "willy-nilly" on the house's southwest corner.

DID YOU KNOW? *During the 1899 remodel of the house, Bishop James Funsten decamped to a mission at the Fort Hall Indian Reservation.*

AT LEFT: *The house is hauled down Warm Springs Avenue to its new home near the Old Pen.*

Lewis and Clark Garden

The Idaho Botanical Garden created its Lewis and Clark Native Plant Garden in 2006 to mark the bicentennial of the Lewis and Clark expedition (1804-1806).

The importance of botany to both explorers is apparent in the number of Western plant species named "clarkia" or "lewisii" — including Idaho's state flower, syringa, or Philadelphus lewisii.

"So we thought, why not create a single snapshot of the plants Lewis and Clark encountered on their journey?" said Julia Rundberg, director of the Botanical Garden.

Staffers perused the explorers' journals and came up with a list of 140 plant species. The Lewis and Clark Garden, which stretches across

PHOTO BY DARIN OSWALD

DID YOU KNOW? *Some of the plants found by Lewis and Clark, including certain orchids, are so delicate and place-specific that they can't survive in Boise. The Idaho Botanical Garden staff is considering different ways to include them — either as photographs or specimens. Pictured here: A bronze sculpture of Sacajawea by Agnes Vincen Talbot. Sacajawea was a Shoshone guide who aided the explorers on their western trek.*

a sunny hillside at the Botanical Garden, includes 125 of those species. The rest are on the garden's wish list.

The garden's collection includes plants native to the range that stretches from Great Falls, Mont., to The Dalles, Ore. Boise sits roughly in the middle.

The staff has recreated four distinct biomes for the collection: prairie, mountain, wetland and coniferous forest — a challenge in the dry desert Foothills where the garden is located.

"We've been able to create microclimates with soil amendments, water, creating shade with rocks and tree canopies," said Rundberg.

Successes include bear grass, which usually prefers growing near glaciers in higher, cooler, wetter regions than Boise.

Bitterroot has been fun to grow, said garden botanist Ann DeBolt, "as long as we can keep the rabbits from

Lewis and Clark first collected cutleaf daisies in the autumn of 1805 along the Clearwater River in Idaho. The flowers grow in the Lewis and Clark Garden in Boise.

eating them."

There are challenges. A Lewis and Clark plant like red mountain heather (Phyllodoce empetriformis) isn't available commercially and probably wouldn't survive in Boise even with gardener intervention, DeBolt said.

Two onion species noted by Lewis and Clark, Geyer's onion and Tolmie's onion (Allium geyeri and Allium tolmiei, respectively), are "in production" in the garden's propaga-

tion bed, said DeBolt. They'll join the collection one day.

Rundberg looks forward to a time when the Lewis and Clark Garden might offer a chance to organize special events — a syringa festival, for example, to capture the brief but fragrant blooming season of Idaho's native.

A syringa fest might not be as showy as lilac festivals in other cities, said Rundberg.

"But it would be our own."

Castle Rock Reserve

Castle Rock, a dramatic outcropping that's part of a 48-acre reserve in the hills above Boise, served as a gathering place for Native Americans from the Shoshone, Bannock and Paiute tribes in the late 19th century.

At that time and before, geothermal springs in the area formed bathing ponds. Historians and tribal members from the Duck Valley and Fort Hall reservations say that Castle Rock (then known as Eagle Rock) was a sacred place used for healing rituals and burials.

In 1990, the East End Neighborhood Association and tribal members started a grass-roots campaign to protect it. The neighborhood association, tribes and the city raised the money in 1995 to buy the Castle

IDAHO STATESMAN FILE

Betty Foster and the Castle Rock monument she helped pay for. For several years, every time a celebration rolled around, Foster's family members donated to a monument fund in lieu of gifts.

Rock land from a developer.

The city named the site Castle Rock Reserve. Officials consulted with tribal members to relocate trails in the area away from possible burial sites. The city worked with neighborhood volunteers and Bureau of Land Management experts to replant

native plant species in the reserve.

Longtime East End resident Betty Foster nominated Castle Rock as a Boise icon. Foster, a former school librarian, led the effort to raise money for a tribute stone to mark the area. The stone stands today near the Bacon Drive entrance to Quarry View Park. It's etched with two eagle feathers in homage to the area's original name and a reminder that this is sacred ground.

The Foothills

DID YOU KNOW? *The Ridge to Rivers system through the Foothills includes 154 trails. Pictured here: lupine, a typical Foothills wildflower.*

PHOTO BY PETE ZIMOWSKY

The Foothills create a sense of enclosure that's intuitive for a native, a sense that's not even conscious until you're in a city without Foothills, where you can't just look up, over the urban skyline, and see rolling shoulders of green, or gold or sage gray or even white, depending on the season.

And no one ever gets jaded about Foothills light. It's as dazzling as anything the Mediterranean has to offer. Witness the photos that pop up on Facebook pages anytime one of those freakish post-storm rainbows appears in a purple sky over Day-Glo chartreuse hills. People try to out-Foothills one another with their cameras.

The subject of Foothills preservation dates to the 1940s, when residents started talking about the fate of the land that had been part of the Boise Army Barracks military training area.

Thanks to the advocacy of a grass-roots coalition and former Mayor Brent Coles, Boise taxpayers in 2001 approved the Foothills serial levy, a two-year property tax.

The tax raised $10 million to buy open space around Boise. The city continues to buy land for preservation.

The 130-mile Ridge to Rivers trail system snakes throughout the Foothills. The city of Boise, Ada County, the Bureau of Land Management's Four Rivers Field Office, the Boise National Forest, and the Idaho Fish and Game Department came together in 1992 to pool money and expertise to maintain the interconnected trails.

The Ridge to Rivers trails offer migrating birds and wildflowers that range from minuscule prairie stars to wild onions to showy lupine. Herds of sheep pass through in the spring on their way to summer grazing areas. The trails offer vistas from so high, Boise appears small enough to carry on a dinner plate.

Writer Cort Conley, director of literature for the Idaho Commission on the Arts, quotes literary critic Cyril Connolly: "No city should be too large for a man to walk out of in a morning."

"And in that regard," says Conley, "the Foothills keep Boise bearable morning, noon and — for coyotes and cougars — night."

Arrowleaf Balsam Root

Walk the hills around Boise in the warm season and you're sure to find certain native plants — white-flowered yarrow with its furry, pungent leaves (mashable into a throat-soothing tea), rabbitbrush and sagebrush. Those bright, early season yellow blooms that look like sunflowers and grow about a foot tall? Chances are they're arrowleaf balsam root (Balsamorhiza sagittata).

The pointed-leafed plant has nutritious seeds and a root that can grow 30 feet deep, said Cyndi Coulter, an analyst with the Idaho Department of Fish and Game. Mashed arrowleaf roots make a wound dressing, she said. They taste bitter, but roots were a food source for Plains tribes, according to "Sagebrush Country" by

PHOTO BY ANNA WEBB

DID YOU KNOW? *The bright blooms of Wyethia, or mule's ears, resemble arrowleaf balsam root, pictured here. The leaves are the giveaway. Mule's ears leaves really look like mule's ears. Arrowleaf leaves really look like arrowheads.*

Ronald J. Taylor.

If you want to try growing the plant in your garden, buy a small one from a nursery specializing in natives. Don't try to dig up one in the Foothills. The long root makes transplanting dicey. And digging up wildflowers is Just. Not. Good.

The arrowleaf balsam root requires

patience. It typically takes several years for a new plant to bloom. But they're long-lived and require little water and care once established.

Here's a beautiful word to add to your plant-word repertoire courtesy of Coulter: Arrowleaf balsam roots "senesce," or go dormant, after seeding in late spring.

Flag on Simplot Hill

Potato magnate J.R. Simplot donated his massive house in the Boise Highlands to the state of Idaho in 2005 for use as a gubernatorial residence. His one stipulation: that the equally massive U.S. flag continue to wave above the house.

True to their word, state officials flew the Simplot flag, even while they were deciding to give the house back to the family because of expenses.

"It's always a picture people want to take, standing under the flag. You can see the flag from anywhere in the valley," said Jennifer Pike of the Department of Administration.

At 30 feet by 50 feet, the flag is among the largest — if not the largest — in the state. If it weren't flying, the flag would fill a 50-gallon drum, Pike said.

As the story goes, after Simplot built the house in 1979, neighbors complained about the sound of the flag flapping in the wind. Some said it sounded like a gunshot.

The billionaire obliged by getting a taller flag pole. It stretches some 200 feet into the air. The height decreased the flapping volume.

The flag has flown at half-staff following the deaths of military personnel in combat, the death of Joe Albertson in 1993, and any other time the president or the governor made a proclamation that flags should be lowered.

The Simplot flag requires monthly repairs.

"The wind whips up there pretty good," said Pike.

The state cycles through three or four flags each year, she added. Each costs $1,800.

IDAHO STATESMAN FILE

DID YOU KNOW? *The famous flag flies over a 7,370-square-foot house and nearly 38 acres, mostly grassy hillside. The latter is one of the most popular, if occasionally dangerous, sledding destinations in town. One pastime: riding ice blocks down the slopes. Pictured here: J.R. Simplot, right, and then-Gov. Dirk Kempthorne on the day Simplot gave the house and its iconic flag to the state.*

Bogus Basin

Several Statesman readers nominated Bogus Basin as a Boise icon, including Andy Miller, who noted the way the ski hill "lights up the sky at night." Indeed, most Boiseans are familiar with the silvery light that shines off the mountain in the winter as headlights snake their way home.

The celebrated Sun Valley Lodge opened its doors in 1936, but Bogus Basin — named for con artists who sold fake gold dust in the area in the late 1880s — wasn't far behind.

Like other building projects in Boise, including the old Ada County Courthouse, Boise Art Museum and the Oregon Trail Memorial Bridge on Capitol Boulevard, Bogus has its roots in the Works Progress Administration, the massive Depression-era public works building program. According to the definitive book

"Building Bogus Basin" by Boise historian Eve Chandler, a WPA road project that began in 1938 opened Bogus as a year-round recreation area.

That was the same year the Boise Ski Club filed its papers of incorporation with the state. Club members had been meeting casually for a few years by then — strapping on hickory skis and careening down the hills at the end of 8th Street and Horseshoe Bend summit.

The Boise Junior Chamber of Commerce decided Boise needed its own ski hill. The group consulted Forest Service experts, including ski champion Alf Engen, who chose the newly accessible Bogus site. The nonprofit Bogus Basin Recreational Association formed in the fall of 1941 and the Bogus Basin Ski Club

sold the resort's first passes for $25.

The bombing of Pearl Harbor put the opening of Bogus Basin on hold for a year, but on Dec. 20, 1942, a 500-foot rope began pulling skiers up the mountain for the first time. An all-volunteer ski patrol stepped up to guard the slopes.

The resort added chair lifts in the '50s, night skiing and a lodge in the '60s, opportunities for physically challenged skiers in the '70s, Nordic trails and a ski program for kids as young as 3 in the '80s, a high-speed quad to replace an old chairlift in the '90s, and a U.S. Freestyle competition in 2002.

Bogus Basin began as a home-grown operation. It remains one.

"Bogus gives back to the community in many ways," said Chandler, "making skiing affordable for almost

DID YOU KNOW? *Bogus opened for night skiing in 1964. A night lift ticket cost $3. It cost Bogus approximately $65 a night to keep the lights on. For a time, Bogus had the longest illuminated ski run in the world.*

PHOTO BY
PETE ZIMOWSKY

everyone, giving free skiing to youth groups and more."

The nonprofit resort's welfare in an era of warmer winters and shorter seasons is something Boiseans take to heart.

The 2012 season was notable for its lack of snow and the latest opening on record for the 70-year-old resort that employs some 700 people. Bogus lovers dressed in snow gear gathered in January that year on the Basque Block for the "Get Louder for Powder" rally. Season pass holders got cheap beer. Companies donated food. Musicians played. The snow obliged, falling in piles on Bogus a few days later.

Warm Springs Avenue

Not long after the city of Boise was platted in 1863, residents were enjoying geothermal springs on the east side of Table Rock. Native tribes had been using the "healing waters" for many years before that. Bathers reached the springs via a dirt wagon track — the predecessor of the grand Warm Springs Avenue we know today.

By 1870, the territorial prison had been built at the foot of Table Rock, increasing traffic on the road. Farms sprung up, too. The Coston and Krall families started growing fruit nearby. Streets in the area still bear their names.

Judge Milton Kelly, editor of the Tri-Weekly Statesman from 1872 to 1889, bought the hot springs near

IDAHO STATESMAN FILE

DID YOU KNOW? *C.W. Moore's house was the first in the nation warmed by geothermal heat.*

Table Rock in 1889. He expanded it into a more commercial operation. Kelly's Hot Springs became a popular destination for Boise's wealthy citizens. The resort served cocktails. It drew the wrath of local temperance crusaders. According to one account, Kelly's was the first place pages looked for their missing lawmaker bosses when the Legislature was in session.

In 1890, men drilled the first hot

water well in town, just west of the penitentiary.

The venture reduced the flows at Kelly's to a warm trickle.

The Artesian Hot and Cold Water Co. started laying hot water pipe along Warm Springs Avenue. According to the Idaho State Historical Society, this was the first documented use of geothermal heat in the U.S. The Idaho Statesman described the natural hot water as "right from Hades."

The water company directors devised a brilliant ploy to use the newly accessible water in the most high-profile way. They opened the Natatorium on Warm Springs not far from the hot water wells in 1892. One writer described the Nat as a "Moorish pleasure palace." With towering ceilings and a two-story copper slide, the place offered residents a huge pool of 98-degree water and a 40-foot lava rock outcropping for diving. Massive potted ferns hung from the ceiling. Visitors could enjoy Turkish baths, smoking rooms and areas designated for lounging.

The Nat had a wooden floor that could be rolled out over the pool for dances. This was an age of superlatives. The largest dance floor in the city — host of lavish gubernatorial balls — was a manifestation of the first geothermal system in a booming capital city.

About the same time, water company board member and First National Bank of Idaho founder C.W. Moore built a new house on Warm Springs Avenue and heated it with natural hot water.

The stylish Queen Anne, which still stands at Warm Springs and Walnut, inspired other affluent Boiseans to follow Moore's lead and build their houses on the hot water line.

The area became so well-known that a 1943 Statesman article quoted humorist Will Rogers referring to Warm Springs Avenue as "hot water bottle boulevard."

The mix of residents on the fashionable avenue included a mining baron, an opera singer, the cousin of celebrated western painter Charles Russell, a law partner of William Borah and many others.

Geothermal heat was a catalyst for other developments. The Boise Rapid Transit Co. built tracks connecting Downtown to the Natatorium. The brick building that houses the Trolley House Restaurant at 1821 Warm Springs marked the end of the rail line.

The old Natatorium met its demise in the 1930s after windstorms damaged it beyond repair. The "new" Nat sits in the footprint of the former pleasure palace. It is now an outdoor public city pool.

The original hot water district still heats hundreds of homes.

Idaho Children's Home

The Rev. O.P. Christian founded the Children's Home Society of Idaho in 1908 to care for and educate Idaho's orphaned, abandoned and neglected children. Cynthia Mann, a teacher and children's activist, donated the property and a six-room house on Warm Springs Avenue as the society's first home. The society built its large sandstone structure on that same site in 1910.

For more than 50 years, the children who passed through the home's doors lived on the building's second floor. There was a room for girls, a room for boys and a room for babies. Other features included outdoor sleeping porches to use during the warm season and an isolated infirmary room accessible only from outside for children with contagious illnesses.

During national crises, both

FROM THE COLLECTION OF MARK BALTES

World Wars and the Great Depression, the home took in children whose parents were living but unable

to care for them. Some returned for their children. Some didn't.

The home changed in 1966 when federal legislation began to favor a foster-care system. Many orphanages across the country closed. The Children's Home transitioned to the treatment facility it is today. Its Warm Springs Counseling Center provides mental, emotional and behavioral health services for at-risk kids and the families that care for them, regardless of their ability to pay.

Remnants of the home's early days remain in the form of more than 6,000 records of the children who lived there over the years. The records, many containing handwrit-ten letters from parents who gave up their children, as well as mementos and photographs, are heart-warming in some cases, heart-rending in others.

Though it hasn't operated as an orphanage for close to 50 years, the home still fields an average of a call a week from someone who was adopted from the home and is looking for family information, staffers say.

The staff will continue to help those callers piece together their personal histories. It also has done its part to preserve the records, many of which are on old and brittle paper. Grants from private donors and the city's Boise 150 program have paid to digitally archive the records.

Sidewalk Stamps

As the Ada County Highway District replaces worn sidewalks in Boise's oldest neighborhoods, the historic stamps — signatures of contractors who laid the concrete — are vanishing icons.

But many are still left around the city's North and East ends, and the Boise Bench. The oldest date to 1908. Some are handwritten. Some include designs, even drawings of trees.

The "gold standard" of sidewalk stamps are the brass stamps left in the 1940s by the Works Progress Administration. Some cities, including San Diego, have policies to preserve their sidewalk markings.

Local photographer Peter Oberlindacher made it his mission to photograph as many sidewalk stamps as possible. The city of Boise bought several of Oberlindacher's photographs for inclusion in the Boise Visual Chronicle, the city's art collection.

DID YOU KNOW? *The Ada County Highway District has saved portions of historic sidewalks and given the chunks of old concrete to residents when they've requested them. The Andrew Sunton stamp at the top is near 6th and Thatcher streets in the North End. The 1940 Works Progress Administration stamp is on 6th Street at Memorial Park.*

PHOTOS BY ANNA WEBB

Stone Steps and Hitching Posts

The stone "steps to nowhere" still found in upscale neighborhoods such as Warm Springs and Harrison Boulevard are remnants of a time when Boiseans got around town by horse-drawn buggy.

The steps date to the late 19th century. They were located near the residences of people who were well-off enough to keep their own carriages or to call them to their homes or offices — the forerunner of taxis.

The sandstone hitching posts that still stand in Boise's oldest neighborhoods are even more common than stone steps.

According to city historians, ownership of these stone remnants is analogous to trees on the county-owned right-of-way strip. They fall

DID YOU KNOW? *You can see a well-preserved stone step etched with the name of its original owner, Dr. Springer, at C.W. Moore Park, 150 S. 5th St. in Downtown Boise. This photo shows a post and steps in the 1300 block of Warm Springs Avenue — it's apt that the steps are near a modern bus stop.*

into a gray zone. They're kind of yours, but you can't take them with you if you move.

Find hitching posts near 10th and Hays streets north of Boise High School, near 1st and 2nd streets, on Harrison Boulevard and on Warm Springs Avenue.

The Greenbelt

Boise wouldn't be Boise without its Foothills, its river or its Greenbelt.

This is intriguing, considering that Boise didn't always love its river.

During the city's first century, the Boise River was a dumping ground for trash, industrial waste and raw sewage — even animal waste from the zoo. The river's banks were foreboding, too, overgrown with brambles.

The city hired California consultants in the mid-1960s who pointed out that the river could become Boise's greatest asset, if it were treated right.

Bill Onweiler, a city councilman at the time, and Gordon Bowen, director of Parks and Recreation from 1956-78, started talking about transforming the ignored stretch along the water into something better.

Onweiler, who died in 2010, Bowen and others even petitioned Sen. Frank Church to secure the first funds to start the project (a stretch of the Greenbelt is now named for Church's widow, public lands advocate Bethine Church).

In 1969, city leaders appointed the city's first Greenbelt and Pathways Committee. For the next three decades, a long line of committee volunteers advised the mayor and council by identifying parcels to buy, working out path designs and finding money.

The committee followed a basic principle that still stirs emotion: "Preserve for the public, in perpetuity, unrestricted access to the river and the special and unique forms of recreation it provides."

With most of the Greenbelt complete, the committee dissolved in 1997.

The city celebrated the Greenbelt's 30th anniversary in 1999. Patti Murphy, public relations coordinator for Parks & Rec at the time, said some of the original committee members came to celebrate. Albertsons baked a 30-foot cake with a map of the Greenbelt in the icing and Idaho Airships took aerial photos. Workers buried a time capsule (held in a baby-sized burial box from Morris Hill Cemetery) near a stone marker east of the former Wheels R Fun building in Shoreline Park. The capsule contains written memories from Boise residents, photos, and letters from then-Gov. Dirk Kempthorne, Mayor Brent Coles and Jim Hall, former director of Boise Parks and Recreation.

The city will open the capsule in 2019, the Greenbelt's 50th anniversary.

PHOTO BY PETE ZIMOWSKY

DID YOU KNOW? *The Greenbelt stretches from Lucky Peak past Garden City. The 2013 opening of Marianne Williams Park (east of the East ParkCenter Bridge) added more pathways to the 25-mile Greenbelt. Pictured here: The portion of the Greenbelt at the west end of Veterans Park during high water season.*

Municipal Park

Municipal Park, one of the leafiest, shadiest and stateliest parks in the city, has a storied past that includes car campers, baseball and something known as the "hobo jungle."

In 1910, the Boise School District bought 25 acres beside the river, where Municipal Park is now. The plan was to build a baseball stadium. Instead, the district leased the land to the Boise Commercial Club. The club opened a tourist campground.

The timing was good. It coincided with a national homesteading surge that brought people to Idaho, especially between the years of 1912 and 1917. According to city historians, the homesteaders came by car, earning the nickname "auto-tramps."

By 1918, the Boise Tourist Park was welcoming thousands of campers a season. The camping fee was 25 cents per car. The park offered amenities, including a communal kitchen with 18 electric hot plates, a laundry with natural geothermal water and an "auto laundry" — cement slabs where people could park for easy car washing. The Idaho Federation of Labor donated a bathhouse to the camp in 1919.

The "urban" camping trend grew. In the years after World War I, 20,000 cars a year came through Boise's tourist camp. The average stay: seven days.

A June 1920 Statesman article noted the hometowns and the destinations of a few campers. They included Dr. W.J. Wilson, traveling from Spokane to New York; A. Gerard, traveling from Boston to Seattle; and A.P. Fryan of Blackfoot,

IDAHO STATESMAN FILE

DID YOU KNOW? *Municipal Park includes a bocce ball court, thanks to the Italian American Club of Boise. In 2008, the club submitted a partnership proposal to the Boise parks department to build the court. The joint effort resulted in a court in the east end of the park — and the inaugural IAC Bocce Tournament in 2008. Ann Morrison and Julia Davis parks now have bocce courts as well.*

headed "anywhere."

The Boise Chamber of Commerce built a communal hall at the tourist park in 1921. The hall featured a screened porch and French doors that opened into a room with a fireplace made of local stone. According to a story in the Statesman, campers spent their evenings sitting by the fireplace or dancing to music provided by a phonograph, aka "talking machine," donated by a local citizen.

Heavy use made it hard for the Boise Commercial Club to maintain the camp. It began a gradual decline in the 1920s. A 1921 article in the Statesman included a blistering review from an Oregon camper who referred to Boise's camp as a "dirty, ragged infant," a place where "mosquitoes revel and feast on the hapless tourist."

In 1927, the city bought the land from the School District and renamed it Municipal Park. Campers continued to spend time there until

NO-128-TOURIST PARK CAMP GROUNDS BOISE IDAHO,

FROM THE COLLECTION OF MARK BALTES

the Great Depression, when public interest in car camping waned and the park earned a reputation as a "hobo jungle."

The city closed the park to camping in 1938. It became a traditional civic park after that, and, to the

delight of baseball fans, the local home of the Pioneer League.

Boise's home team played under several names, including the Pilots, the Yankees and finally the Braves until 1963, the Pioneer League's final season.

Lonesome Larry

Two decades ago the sockeye destined to become one of the most famous salmon in the West took a solitary 900-mile swim up the Columbia and Snake rivers.

An easy trip? No way. It presented obstacles that would have stopped a less hale fish: 6,500 feet in elevation gain; hungry eagles, bobcats and bears, not to mention eight dams standing in the way.

The sockeye's aim: returning to Redfish Lake to spawn. He made it, but no other sockeye did. Just one year before, in 1991, the federal government had added sockeye to its endangered species list.

Allyson Coonts, the 7-year-old daughter of a Sawtooth Hatchery technician, named the single sockeye Lonesome Larry.

Scientists intervened. They

PHOTO BY DARIN OSWALD

captured Larry. They extracted his milt and used it to fertilize eggs laid by female fish in 1996 and 1997.

In the following years, more fish made it back to Redfish. Nearly 250 came in 2012. That was better than solitary Larry, but nothing like the 1880s, when as many as 35,000 salmon came each year — so many that someone considered building a cannery at the lake.

The ultimate success of Lonesome

Larry's and biologists' efforts is unknown. The dams that make salmon migration so tough remain in place. Redfish Lake sockeye remain on the federal endangered species list.

Lonesome Larry was sacrificed in the milt harvesting process. He's been stuffed and hangs on a wall at the MK Nature Center. He's a popular attraction among visitors. Some of his milt is still on ice, capable of fathering more fish.

DID YOU KNOW?

Lonesome Larry has his own Facebook page. It describes him as sleek, slim, fire engine red and plenty virile. His personal interests include "long romantic conversations with fisheries biologists" and "fleeing predators."

Pioneer Cemetery

The oldest legible grave marker in Pioneer Cemetery on Warm Springs Avenue is that of a little girl.

Carrie Logan, age 5 years, 11 months and five days, died in the summer of 1864. Her father, Thomas Logan, became mayor of Boise 10 years later. Mayor Logan, too, is buried in Pioneer. It is the oldest cemetery in continuous use in the city of Boise.

The land was a public burial ground until 1872, when its owner, John Krall (a street in the area still bears his name), sold it to the Masons and the Independent Order of Odd Fellows.

The city took over maintenance in 1920. The cemetery fell into disrepair in the next decades. Someone stole its fence. Vandals damaged headstones.

The state's centennial in 1990 inspired the Boise Metro Rotary Club and the city to restore Pioneer Cemetery. Scores of Boise residents with compelling stories are buried there. They include Corilla Robbins, who died in 1927. Robbins came to Idaho in an ox cart and led the women's suffrage movement in the state. She was a woman of "firsts." She rode in the first airplane and the first car to arrive in Boise. Robbins also owned the first residential telephone in the city.

Judge Milton Kelly, editor and publisher of the Idaho Statesman and owner of Kelly's Hot Springs on the edge of town, was buried there in 1892. Kelly was a member of the first session of the Idaho Territorial Legislature and helped draft its first laws.

Plots are still available at Pioneer for about $2,000 apiece.

PHOTO BY ANNA WEBB

DID YOU KNOW? *Pioneer Cemetery reveals the ethnic mix of Boise's early settlers. Pictured here: A headstone written in Hebrew for a child who died in 1871. The cemetery contains the graves of many children, including that of a 6-year-old boy who died in 1878. The inscription reads: "Papa, we will occupy the house together. Yes, my son, we will."*

Jesus Urquides Gravesite

PHOTO FROM THE JESUS URQUIDES MEMORIAL

The headstone, etched with the word "Papa," stands in the Pioneer Cemetery, near the fence on the Warm Springs Avenue side. Jesus Urquides was born in Mexico in 1833. He came to the Boise area from California, drawn by the discovery of gold in the Boise Basin in 1863.

Urquides became a mule packer of great renown. He brought supplies to mining camps in Silver City, Atlanta, Challis and other Idaho towns.

According to one story in Max Delgado's biography, "Jesus Urquides: Idaho's Premier Muleteer," Urquides once figured out how to carry a nearly two-mile-long steel cable to Central Idaho. Cutting the cable wasn't an option, so he wound it into a huge coil and attached it to the backs of 35 mules arranged in three rows.

In 1879, Urquides inherited land at 115 Main St. Fellow Mexican-born muleteers settled nearby. By the 1930s, more than 35 cabins stood in the area. Boiseans knew the neighborhood as Urquides Village or Spanish Village. Urquides died there in 1928 at the age of 92. After a fire in the early 1970s damaged several homes in the village, the city condemned them and demolished the neighborhood.

The Jesus Urquides Memorial, an outdoor installation by Dwaine Carver near the former village at Main and 1st streets, includes sculptural pieces, interpretive plaques and a bronze rendition of an old-time camera with Urquides' image. And note, when you sit in the city bus shelter near the Urquides Memorial,

DID YOU KNOW? *Maria Dolores Urquides Binnard, Urquides' daughter, lived in Urquides Village. She promoted the neighborhood as a tourist attraction, led tours and shared her own stories with visitors. She decorated her father's grave each Dia de los Muertos until her death in 1965. Community members revived the tradition in 2006. The gravesite is the scene of a remembrance celebration each year.*

PHOTO AT RIGHT BY JOE JASZEWSKI

it's the muleteer's face rendered in graphic red and white that's shading you.

Bureau of Reclamation Building

The unassuming brick building on Broadway Avenue played a key role in irrigating large areas of Southern Idaho and southeastern Oregon.

Built in 1912, it was the headquarters for the Bureau of Reclamation's Boise Irrigation Project. Engineers and administrators managed major construction works — including Arrowrock Dam, Boise's canal systems and Diversion Dam — from the building.

During the Arrowrock project, the building also served as a stop for a private railroad spur for deliveries to the construction site.

The building was the first permanent office for Reclamation in the area. The agency occupied the Broadway site for decades. In the summer of 2003, it moved to larger offices, making the old building's

PHOTO BY ANNA WEBB

DID YOU KNOW? *The Reclamation Building is Craftsman style with low, hipped dormers and a large porch. The style was popular for residential architecture in the early 1900s but was mainly used in the public sphere for resource-related agencies.*

future uncertain. In 2006, the bureau transferred ownership to the Idaho State Historical Society.

The building's interior is largely intact, said Dan Everhart of Preservation Idaho. That includes original woodwork, doorways, hardware,

several safes and an original urinal in the men's room.

One cool original feature: a bank teller window in the lobby. Workers lined up at this window to get their paychecks after putting in their hours on Reclamation's many projects.

Boise Little Theater

Boise Little Theater started presenting plays in a theater at Gowen Field in 1948. That was the same year Israel and Pakistan declared independence, the Hells Angels motorcycle gang formed in California and Arturo Toscanini made his television debut with an all-Wagner program.

Since then, BLT casts have performed everything from "Dracula" to "Arsenic and Old Lace." The former involved complicated illusions with smoke, mirrors and a real German shepherd playing the role of a wolf. The latter has graced the stage no fewer than three times. It was the first play performed in 1948. The group revived it for its 25th and 50th seasons.

The group's darkest era came in

IDAHO STATESMAN FILE

DID YOU KNOW? *Boise Little Theater is one of the oldest all-volunteer community theaters in the country.*

1957, when a fire killed two BLT members and burned the Gowen Field theater.

The community rallied to build the troupe's distinctive, dome-shaped home on Fort Street soon after. Noted local architect Art Troutner designed the theater pro bono, using then-innovative curved laminated beams as structural elements. Other community members donated building materials and sweat equity. According to theater literature, Troutner often brought clients to the theater to show off his construction techniques.

The theater is known for its devoted membership, including those who have been with the troupe since its earliest years. A plaque memorializing the two men who died in the Gowen fire hangs in the Fort Street lobby.

Fort Boise

In the 1860s, pioneers were traveling en masse through the Boise Valley on the Oregon Trail. Others came through on their way to the Boise Basin in search of gold or to the Owyhees in search of silver. The U.S. Army saw a need to protect them.

The Army sent Maj. Pinckney Lugenbeel to establish a cavalry post in the area. He chose the location where Fort Boise sits today just north of Downtown.

The fort, known by various names through the years, including Camp Boise and Boise Barracks, opened on July 4, 1863.

Lugenbeel hired scores of civilians to build the fort, said historian and preservationist John Bertram. At one point, 138 builders and craftsmen were working at the site — more than the 125 enlisted men stationed there.

PHOTO PROVIDED BY PRESERVATION IDAHO

DID YOU KNOW? *The 1863 surgeon's quarters, sometimes called the quartermaster building or Building 4, is one of the oldest structures on the site. For the fort's 150th anniversary, the VA Medical Center partnered with Preservation Idaho on a plan to restore the building's exterior and rehabilitate its fireplace room to the post–Civil War period.*

The Army's need for labor, building materials and food helped the city of Boise prosper in its earliest days, said Bertram.

Fort Boise grew fast. By the fall of 1864, it had 19 buildings plus parade grounds. The Army stationed troops in Boise for several decades, until the years leading up to World War I. In 1912, the Army began relocating troops and using the fort to train horses for the cavalry.

During World War I, the character of Fort Boise began to shift from military to medical as soldiers on horseback became obsolete and the Red Cross and others campaigned to use the site as a military rehabilitation hospital. In 1920, the U.S. Public Health Service opened a tuberculosis hospital there.

President Franklin Roosevelt transferred control of the site to the Veterans Administration (now the Department of Veterans Affairs) in 1938.

The old fort is now home to the Boise VA Medical Center. The Idaho State Veterans Home is also part of the complex. Much of the original fort property became city recreation land.

Fort Boise, like the city of Boise, marked its sesquicentennial in 2013. The site has been a focal point for preservation groups since the beginning of the 20th century, when local clubs, including the Columbian

PHOTO PROVIDED BY IDAHO STATE HISTORICAL SOCIETY, 60-1.57

DID YOU KNOW? *This is the oldest known photo of Fort Boise, taken just after the Civil War, about 1870. Building 1, at right, is still standing on Officers Row. The porch no longer exists.*

Club and others, petitioned the War Department to save the fort's old structures.

The campus is in the National Register of Historic Places and still includes dozens of buildings related to military and medical history. Large brick residences from the early 1900s line the upper drive known as Officers Row.

A few structures date to the fort's — and the city's — first years, creating a collection of buildings

unlike any other.

Fort Boise is the second fort with that name. The British Hudson's Bay Co. built a fort, which was more of a trading post, in 1834 near the confluence of the Boise and Snake rivers near present-day Parma.

Hudson's Bay built the fort to compete with Fort Hall, a trading post near what's now Pocatello. The fur trade declined and the original Fort Boise became a supply point on the Oregon Trail.

Fort Boise Military Reserve Cemetery

Stroll through the Military Reserve Cemetery on a moonlit night and you'll find yourself in one of the city's most somber landscapes.

The cemetery has been on the hillside above Boise since 1906, when the U.S. Army relocated it from its original site about a half-mile down Mountain Cove Road.

Burials began at the original location in 1863, the year Fort Boise opened, said Ken Swanson, executive director of the Idaho Military History Museum. It was a military cemetery, but civilians including men and women who died traveling the Oregon Trail are buried there, too.

Floods were always a concern. A particularly bad flash flood from Cottonwood Creek in 1906 inspired officers at the fort to hire contractors to relocate the cemetery to higher ground.

The job was supposed to take one year, said Swanson. It took three because no one knew the full extent of burials. Wooden headstones had been lost through the years, making identification a challenge. In the end, the workers moved 166 graves.

The Boise Barracks closed in 1913, and burials stopped.

After World War II, the Department of Veterans Affairs began closing a number of small cemeteries across the U.S. to save money. The Army didn't want to take on the responsibility of moving the graves once again and asked that the cemetery remain where it was. The VA deeded it to the city of Boise in 1947 as a historic site.

The cemetery fell into disrepair in the following decades, until the

Idaho Civil War Volunteers stepped up in the 1990s.

"We got together, adopted it and started taking care of it," said Swanson, a member of the group.

That care included replacing broken headstones and providing the labor to put them up.

DID YOU KNOW? *247 enlisted men, officers, their family members and civilians are buried at the cemetery. The military personnel include veterans from the Mexican War (1846-1848), Indian Wars (late 1860s through 1870s in Idaho), Spanish-American War (1898) and the Civil War (1861-1865).*

PHOTOS BY JOE JASZEWSKI

Long after the barracks closed, people continued to discover graves at the original cemetery site. In 1998, flood-control excavation turned up one full grave and the remains of two others.

The Idaho Civil War Volunteers built simple wooden caskets. They held a Memorial Day burial ceremony that year for the three at the Military Reserve Cemetery.

Since it was likely the bodies were those of Civil War veterans, the ceremony followed the Army's 1863 burial protocol for enlisted men.

James A. McClure Federal Building and U.S. Courthouse

It must have been an interesting transition in 1965 when the federal court moved from the 1900s-era stone and brick building at 8th and Bannock to the new courthouse at Fort and 6th streets.

For a time, said Dan Everhart of Preservation Idaho, some considered placing the new courthouse on the land that's now Capitol Park just south of the Statehouse. Business leaders liked the idea of keeping workers and their wallets in the Downtown core. Officials settled instead on a corner of the Military Reserve on Fort Street, where the federal government already owned land.

The building was on trend with the mid-20th century fashions of its time. Its sleek international style features clean lines and lots of glass.

This complex is all about attention to architectural detail. Note the structure in the north parking lot that houses the building's mechanical systems. It echoes the grid pattern on the larger building. The building's entrance is a post 9-11 addition.

Third-generation Boise architect Charles Hummel partnered with a Los Angeles firm to design the building.

The courthouse's exterior walls are not structural. They appear suspended, dramatic. Interviewed by the Statesman in 2006, Hummel said:

"We wanted the building to assert itself, not to be comfortable. It's a challenging building. That's the idea. If a U.S. courthouse doesn't assert itself, it's not much of a courthouse."

The building was named for Sen. James McClure in 2001. McClure died in 2011.

DID YOU KNOW? *Architect Charles Hummel intended that for all its modern style, the building would relate to its surroundings. Massive first floor windows allow a 360-degree view of the surrounding neighborhood, including Fort Boise and the O'Farrell Cabin — the city's oldest structures.*

PHOTO BY JOE JASZEWSKI

O'Farrell Cabin

The O'Farrell Cabin is the oldest family home in Boise. And like the city and Fort Boise, it turned 150 in 2013.

John O'Farrell arrived in New York City from Ireland in 1843. After serving in the British Navy and earning a medal of valor in the Crimean War, he returned to the U.S. and became a prospector. In 1863, he and his wife, Mary, traveled to the Boise Valley by wagon, said city historians.

In June of that year, just weeks before pioneers platted Boise's first 10 blocks, O'Farrell cleared land on what's now Fort Street and built his cabin out of cottonwoods. According to old maps, the cabin originally sat across the street from where it is now, just east of the U.S. Courthouse on Fort Street.

The O'Farrells became prominent citizens. Mary was responsible for the first Catholic services in Boise after she noticed priests passing by the cabin and asked them in. Clergymen held services at the cabin for several years.

John O'Farrell was one of the original investors in the New York Canal and served a term in the Idaho Territory Legislature. The O'Farrells eventually moved out of the cabin into a frame house before moving into the large white brick house that stands today at the corner of 5th and Franklin streets. The couple raised seven children and adopted seven more. They would have been able to see their old cabin from their back window.

The cabin has had many owners. In 1910, the O'Farrell children

PHOTO BY JOE JASZEWSKI

DID YOU KNOW? *When the O'Farrells built their cabin, they chinked the spaces between the cottonwood logs with small branches and clay, said city historians. They covered the inside walls with fabric. The floor was dirt until O'Farrell covered it with planks in 1864. The cabin stands near an incongruous neighbor — the U.S. Federal Building, a classic of modern, mid-20th century style.*

donated it to the Daughters of the American Revolution. In 1957, own-

DID YOU KNOW? *The cabin's simple interior includes wide plank walls and floors, as well as its original fireplace.*

ership passed to the Sons and Daughters of the Idaho Pioneers, then to the city.

In 1999, third-generation Boise architect Charles Hummel and the Columbian Club, one of the city's oldest service clubs, organized a drive to restore the cabin. The city's Millennium Fund also contributed.

In 2002, at a cost of $51,000, craftsmen returned the cabin to its 1912 condition, down to its roof shingles and original paint colors.

Cottonwood Trees

The black cottonwood is one of the few native trees in the Treasure Valley. If you believe the legend about how Boise got its name, a French hunting party came west from the desert in 1833. Seeing green after a long trek through sagebrush, the Frenchmen exclaimed, "Les bois, les bois!"

The trees they saw were cottonwoods and willows growing along what became the Boise River, said Debbie Cook, Boise City arborist.

Cottonwoods, Populus trichocarpa, grow near the water. They rely on river flows, as well as wind to carry their distinctive, fluffy seed pods to germinate. The presence of dams has changed the river through the years and created challenges for cottonwoods, said Cook.

Many cottonwoods now more often reproduce by suckers instead of seeds. Suckers are clones, offering less genetic diversity. Local organizations are trying to help, including Trout Unlimited, which started experimenting with replanting efforts in 2008. The Idaho Botanical Garden is tending 200 black cottonwood trees grown from seed for the Land Trust of the Treasure Valley, said botanist Ann DeBolt. The trust will plant them in the wild when the trees are old enough. Cook's office also enlists volunteers to wrap trunks of young trees that grow along the Greenbelt to protect them from beavers.

Cottonwoods enhance habitat for a great variety of wildlife, said DeBolt. The trees develop cavities in their trunks that are nesting places for certain bird species.

Lewis and Clark made canoes from cottonwoods. Boise's settlers used them to build the city's earliest structures. The wood from cottonwoods is soft. Few of the city's first buildings remain. The O'Farrell Cabin on Fort Street is a rare exception.

Beyond all of this, cottonwoods offer a certain romance.

For one, there's the smell of their buds. How do you even describe something that is so omnipresent and familiar that you don't know you know it? It's that perfume, sticky-sweet some say, that hits you when you ride your bike through Julia Davis Park at dusk.

"I've collected buds in the winter and spring before they open. I keep them in an earthenware pot," said Cyndi Coulter with the Idaho Department of Fish and Game. "Years

DID YOU KNOW? *Cole Porter's song "Don't Fence Me In" includes the line, "Listen to the murmur of the cottonwood trees ..." The song is from a poem by a Montana man, Bob Fletcher, who sold the rights to Porter.*

PHOTO BY DARIN OSWALD

later, the rich, vanilla aroma persists."

In "Magpie Rising: Sketches from the Great Plains," writer Merrill Gilfillan described cottonwoods as trees with "unpretentious dignity" capable of creating "a cool psychological harbor."

Black cottonwoods can grow to 100 feet tall and live for more than 100 years.

In 2013, when Boise marked its 150th anniversary and moved toward its second century, Gilfillan's words rang true about the city's native tree:

"Where there is any hope at all, there are cottonwoods on the horizon."

Happy birthday, hometown.

Alphabetical Index

Categorical Index

Warm Springs Ave., Boise, I[d]

Colophon

The majority of type in this book is set in Adobe Caslon Pro, a font created by Carol Twombly based on William Caslon's typeface designed in 1722. Caslon's font was based on seventeenth-century Dutch old style designs. Because of its practicality, Caslon quickly became popular in Europe and the American Colonies; Benjamin Franklin rarely used any other typeface. The first printings of the American Declaration of Independence and the U.S. Constitution were set in Caslon.

Supporting type is set in Copperplate, designed in 1901 by Frederic W. Goudy. Display type is set in OL Egmont, designed by Dennis Ortiz-Lopez in 2005.

This book is printed on 80-pound Titan dull paper that is FSC-certified (made from pulp from replenished forests). It contains 10 percent post-consumer waste and is acid-free.

The cover is printed on Candesce paper, a 12 pt. coverstock coated on one side. It was manufactured by Clearwater Paper's facility in Lewiston.

The book was printed by Caxton Printers, 312 Main Street, Caldwell. It was bound by Pacific Press Publishing, 1350 North Kings Road, Nampa.

The following Idaho Statesman employees produced this book: writer Anna Webb; designer Lindsie Bergevin; copy editors Jim Keyser, Genie Arcano and Holly Anderson; photographers Joe Jaszewski, Darin Oswald, Katherine Jones, Kyle Green and Pete Zimowsky; photo technician Susanna Smith; news assistant Pat Carson; and Editor Vicki S. Gowler.

Dan Everhart of Preservation Idaho provided research and editing assistance. Mark Baltes provided many of the historic Boise postcards seen throughout the book.

Historian Brandi Burns with the Boise Department of Arts and History and Barbara Perry Bauer with Preservation Idaho shared their time and knowledge for this project.

Preservation Idaho, Boise City Department of Arts and History and Icon Credit Union partnered with the Idaho Statesman to publish this book.

The 100 block of Main Street (formerly part of Warm Springs Avenue) looking east. FROM THE COLLECTION OF MARK BALTES

Some things change.
Our commitment to serving our members never will.

Then...

Now...

150 Boise icons are highlighted in this book, but there are thousands of amazing stories that create the history of our city. Icon Credit Union is proud to have helped bring 150 of the best ones to your fingertips. Enjoy!

IconCreditUnion.org/History

icon
credit union